BATHAMPTON DOWN
A Hill Divided

Front cover: The photographer's twin sons looking across the old quarry workings from the north-east end of Bushy Norwood, c1920s. (© Bath in Time – Dafnis Collection)

Back cover: View over the old quarry workings with Batheaston and Bathford in the distance, c1920s. (© Bath in Time – Dafnis Collection)

Bath, from Hampton Rocks.
(From a painting by A Heaton Cooper, c1927)

BATHAMPTON DOWN
A Hill Divided

1700 – 2000

Researched and Written
by
MARY CLARK

Compiled by
GILLIAN HUGGINS

BATHAMPTON LOCAL HISTORY
RESEARCH GROUP

Published 2017 by Ex Libris Press in association with
Bathampton Local History Research Group

Origination by Ex Libris Press
Bradford-on-Avon
www.ex-librisbooks.co.uk

Printed by CPI Anthony Rowe
Chippenham, Wiltshire

© Bathampton Local History Research Group

ISBN 978-1-91202067-6

British Library Cataloguing-in-Publication Date:
A catalogue record for this book is available from the British Library

CONTENTS

Dedication

To Arthur Green, a 'Bathampton Boy'
whose keen interest in, and extensive knowledge
of the history of the village inspired this book.

Also to my mother, Florence Urch,
who loved Bathampton Down.

Acknowledgements

I wish to thank all those who have been involved
in the production of this book and in particular the following
for their support and for making their resources available.

The Trustees of the Miller Trust, Bathampton without whose
generosity this publication could not have been achieved

The Chairman and Members of Bathampton Parish Council

Colin Johnston and staff at Bath Record Office
Ann Buchanan and staff of Bath Central Library
The Staff of Somerset Archives and Local Studies Service
Stuart Burroughs, Bath at Work Museum
Daniel Brown, Bath in Time
Victoria Art Gallery, Bath and North East Somerset Council
Wiltshire and Swindon History Centre
Bristol Record Office
Bristol Reference Library
British Newspaper Archive
Bob Millard and William Mannings
Sheila Edwards, Cath Field, Terry Clark
Trish Turner and John Pemberton
Members of the Bathampton Local History Research Group
including Gill Huggins, Cecilia Parkes, Rosemary Dyer
Deirdre Bryant and Crystal Payne

FOREWORD

Historic landscape interpretation is a tricky thing. Trying to make sense of all those lumps and bumps on the ground, matching maps to documentary sources isn't easy. So why do we do it? Why do we isolate a geographical plot and investigate its development when we can enjoy and appreciate it knowing nothing? This is the question any local historian has to answer before starting any project and is at the essence of landscape history.

Curiosity would be one reason, I suppose, but more importantly, at least for me, is the need to put our lives into an historical context, to know about those who came before us and how their lives contrast with our own. Our ancestors looked like us, thought like us, walked the land we walk and help us make sense of our own lives.

In the film *A Canterbury Tale*, actor Eric Portman, who appropriately plays a Kentish local historian, explains his perspective. On describing, to a lecture hall of soldiers, about medieval pilgrims coming to a high ridge in his own village overlooking Canterbury, he says – '*They climbed the hill as you might, they paused for breath as you would and when I stand there I'm only seeing what they saw. We are so close to these people, that I only feel I need to turn my head to see them there beside me*'.

There is a further need to find out more for those of us who know Bathampton Down as our own histories are played out against the development of the area under study. I was brought up in a house in St George's Hill and Bathampton Down was an uphill sort of playground. The trees of the Fussells were a background to our terraced garden. The steep path through the woodland to the upland of golf course and Celtic fields was one I took regularly and the streams which fed the village of Bathampton below were ineffectively dammed with sticks and stones and redirected by my friends and family. Picnics interrupted by cows and a first experience of camping out in a tent on the Down recalled Enid Blyton and, in the woodlands, fairy tales.

The tireless work of local historians, which brings so much more to an appreciation of any place, and their works, amongst which this book should be included, must always be applauded. For those familiar with Bathampton Down, or not, this should act as an inspiration – as it has to me – to go out and explore again, or for the first time, the hillside and hilltop.

This book will help in the reading of this unique landscape farmed and quarried over centuries. All of us who have enjoyed this space without, in our younger years, knowing much about it, can now find, within these pages, everything we need to know.

Stuart Burroughs
Director
Museum of Bath at Work
June 2017

PREFACE

Bathampton Down has a unique history covering some 3,000 years. Evidence of its pre-history, particularly its use for agricultural purposes, can be seen in the extensive archaeological remains that exist on the plateau and surrounding slopes. This period has been comprehensively recorded[1] but little has been written of the Down's more recent history and this has led Mary Clark and Gillian Huggins of the Bathampton Local History Research Group to put together the story of the Down from the Middle Ages to the present time. During this period the hilltop continued to be used for agriculture – mainly the grazing of sheep as the thin, poor, stony soil was unsuitable for anything else. It has also been enjoyed by those who came to picnic, 'take the air' and enjoy the panoramic views.

Today the whole hilltop is generally referred to as Bathampton Down but this has not always been the case for in the early 1700s a wall was built which divided it into two sections - Hampton Warren and Hampton Down. This suggested the structure for the majority of the book, in which the history of each part has been recorded in a methodical way.

Part One tells the story of Hampton Warren where rabbits were bred commercially and there once stood an old house where a jealous husband murdered his wife. Later, Ralph Allen built a folly on the same site surrounded by plantations of fir trees, here the citizens of Bath went to watch prize-fights and celebrated famous victories with fêtes and fireworks. More recently the Bath Golf Club built their clubhouse nearby and constructed their original golf course on the Warren.

Part Two covers the area that was known as Hampton Down which is possibly even more interesting. Here there are remains of once prosperous stone quarries which had an early tramway that led down to the canal below. In one of the caves that formed part of the quarries the body of a young woman was found – a murder which was never solved. In another a secret war time organization had its headquarters. Near the quarries was a rifle range used by the Volunteers before the First World War and to the south-west a famous duel was fought.

Then follows an account of more recent times, after the wall had fallen into disuse, and to conclude a 'Postscript' which records stone features and curiosities on the Down.

We hope that this history will be of interest not only to local residents, many of whom will know Bathampton Down well, but also to those from further afield.

Bathampton Local History Research Group
June 2017

SETTING THE SCENE

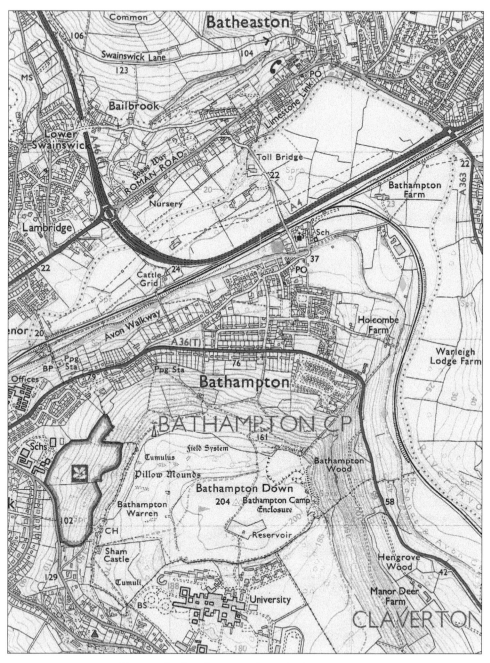

The parish of Bathampton from Ordnance Survey
Explorer Map 155 dated 1997.
(Reproduced under Ordnance Survey licence number 100057966)

1

'To understand things as they are we must understand how they came to be what they are.'

G O Sayles

INTRODUCING BATHAMPTON DOWN

The parish of Bathampton is situated in Somerset, to the north-east of the City of Bath, and covers some 932 acres of which approximately 230 are known today as Bathampton Down – the hill which forms the southern most part of the parish.

The River Avon marks the parish boundaries on the north and east sides and the land rises from the flat fertile meadows of the valley bottom to the steeply rising ground of the hill on the southern side. The summit of the hill forms a plateau which, at its highest point, reaches a height of 669 feet above sea level. It marks the end of a much larger, continuous, plateau comprised of similar 'Downs' that encircle the south side of Bath. They run from Southdown, in the south-west, through to Odd Down, Combe Down and Claverton Down, terminating with Bathampton Down at the most north-easterly point. They are comprised mainly of Oolitic Limestone laid down some 165 million years ago when the whole area was covered by the sea. This stone has been extensively quarried over many centuries – an occupation which has had much influence on the overall landscape and gave rise to the eastern promontory often being referred to as Hampton Cliffs or Hampton Rocks. From the hill top a wide panorama of views opens up taking in the Mendips to the south-west around to the Wiltshire Downs in the far south-east. The vista includes not only the City of Bath but also the many hills and valleys that lie to the east, the River Avon winding through the Avon valley with its adjoining villages, and a birds-eye view of the village of Bathampton itself.

In his *History and Antiquities of Somerset* (published in 1791) John Collinson wrote a description of the parish which included the following:

> 'A considerable part of the hill which rises southeast from the street* is in this parish, and is called Hampton-down. It contains many springs, and produces excellent sheep-feed; but on account of the thinness of the stratum of earth, which in many parts scarcely covers the rock, it is incapable of cultivation. The eastern part of this hill, called the Cliffs, is at least six hundred feet above the river, and from its rocks and steepness is almost inaccessible. Its brow is finely contrasted by rugged projecting rocks and quarries, and by plantations of firs, beneath which fine hanging coppice woods extend almost to the bottom. From this elevated spot the prospects are truly romantic and beautifully diversified'.
> [*Today's High Street].

The whole of the Bathampton Down plateau and its immediate slopes are covered with archaeological remains giving evidence that man was utilizing the area from at least 3,000 years ago. The summit is the site of one of the largest known Iron Age enclosures. Its bank and ditch surrounds an area of about 80 acres, thought to have been used for keeping stock, fairs and trading.

Fig. 1 Aerial view, looking south, of the plateau and north facing slopes of Bathampton Down, showing the Celtic field system, Iron Age enclosure, Bath Golf Course, the 'V' shaped Hampton Down Reservoir and Seven Sisters Quarry.

(Courtesy of P Scilly, 1999)

The Down also contains the remains of a Celtic field system which can be traced over the whole of the plateau and down the surrounding hillside. Banks, which are evidence of the walls of this, can still be clearly seen as they criss-cross the present golf course and the fields below. They are especially noticeable when the sun is low throwing deep shadows outlining their pattern.

In 1857 the Reverend Scarth, Rector of Bathwick and a keen antiquarian, reported seeing the remains of two stone circles, approached by avenues of stones, near the north-west entrance to the enclosure but no trace of these can be found today. There are, however, traces of seven Bronze Age Barrows on the Down, most of which can still be seen.

These were excavated during the early 1800s by the Reverend John Skinner of Camerton who supervised their opening with pickaxes; remains of burials, pottery and animal bones were found. No associated living accommodation has been discovered, but it is possible to see the outline of a small Roman Farm, which perched on the edge of the escarpment looking out over the valley and the village.

There is evidence of the land to the north-west of Bathampton church being occupied from the Iron Age and it is probable that those early occupants were making use of the Down and may have been involved in building the enclosure.

The boundaries of the parish today are much the same as described in the Saxon Charter of 956. From c945 Hantone, or Hampton (as Bathampton was known) was mostly administered by the Monastery of St Peter and St Paul, Bath. King Henry VIII dissolved the Monastery in 1539 and Hampton Manor passed to the crown. What happened after this is unclear but it is recorded that in 1548 Bishop William Barlow yielded it up to King Edward VI who in 1553 sold it to William Crouch, of Wellow. After this the Manor Estate continued to be administered by a succession of Lords of the Manor until it was sold in 1921 when its properties and land passed into private ownership.

The Lord of the Manor who probably had the most impact on the Down was the famous Ralph Allen – business man, entrepreneur and local benefactor. He made his fortune reorganizing the postal service and put it to good use when he became involved in the building of Georgian Bath by opening local quarries and promoting the use of Bath Stone.

Known as the 'Benevolent Man', he did many good works including giving money towards the construction of the Mineral Water Hospital in Bath. He built a mansion for himself at Prior Park, taking up residence in 1741, and then expanded his estate by purchasing the Manor of Bathampton in 1743 and that of Claverton which he finally purchased in 1758.

During the period 1740-64 he created a plan of his holdings entitled *A Survey of the Manours of Hampton, Claverton with Widcombe belonging to Ralph Allen Esq.*[1] This is generally referred to as 'Ralph Allen's Estate Map' and has accompanying Schedules detailing tenants, acreages and land usage. These are held by the Bath Record Office and are the earliest records to be found of the Manor Estate of Hampton. As such they have proved invaluable in understanding the parish's history.

Lords of Bathampton Manor since the Dissolution

1553 – 1586	William Crouch of Wellow and Englishcombe
1586 – 1608	Walter Crouch (Will proved 26 August 1608)
1608 – 1608	William Crouch (buried 10 August 1608)
1608 – 1617	Walter Crouch
c1617 – c1630	Thomasine Olfield
c1630 – 1656	William Bassett II of Claverton
1656 – 1693	William Bassett III (Sir) of Claverton
1693 – 1700	In hands of the Receiver
1701 – 1706	Richard Holder of Claverton
1706 – 1743	Charles Holder
1743 – 1764	Ralph Allen of Prior Park (and Claverton from 1758)
1766 – 1785	Phillip Allen II
1785 – 1850	George Edward Allen
1850 – 1887	Ralph Shuttleworth Allen (Major)
1887 – 1910	Ralph Edward Allen (Major General)
1910 – 1921	Henry Allen who sold the Estate in 1921

The Civil War saw Sir William Waller's troops of some seven thousand Parliamentarians encamped on Bathampton Down, Claverton Down and Odd Down for three weeks during June 1643 – prior to the Battle of Lansdown. Some action was seen during this period, both from the hilltop and the valley bottom, with the Parliamentarians attacking Sir Ralph Hopton's Royalist forces as they advanced along the Bathford side of the Avon Valley, intent on capturing Bath. In July 1645 the area was also a venue for the assembling of troops prior to the siege of Bristol.

The Down was used for agricultural purposes continually from early man to the end of the 19th century. In 1881 the Bath Golf Club started to rent part of the hill top for use as a golf course and for a time this existed alongside the grazing of animals. The 1921 sale enabled the Golf Club to purchase the whole of Bathampton Down and gradually major alterations began to take place with the greater part of the plateau being changed from agricultural use to amenity use as the course was established. To a great extent, this move safeguarded the archaeological remains whilst the central area has become legally protected by being listed as a scheduled monument of national importance. The Down as a whole is now also designated as an Area of Outstanding Natural Beauty. The Bath Golf Club continues to thrive and limited grazing takes place on some of the remaining land.

An earlier change, however, took place when, during the beginning of the 1700s, the Lord of the Manor of Bathampton split the Down into two parts and the western remains of the Iron Age enclosure were used as part of a dividing wall. Thus began a series of changes and events that have extended the fascinating story of the Down through to the twenty-first century.

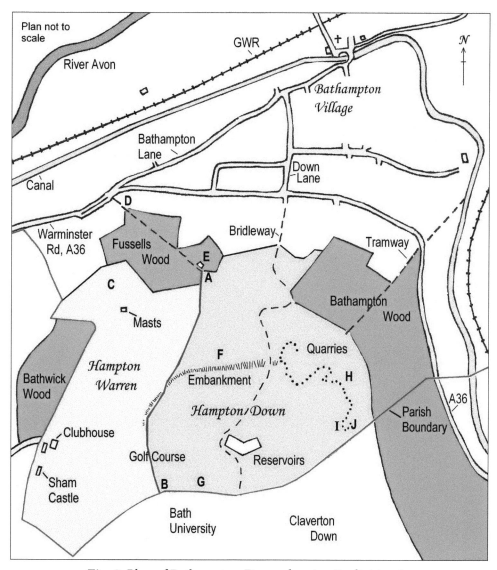

Fig. 2 Plan of Bathampton Down showing its division into Hampton Warren and Hampton Down with past and present sites referred to in the book. (M F Clark, 2016)

Key: A – B   Remains of Dividing Wall
       C   Warren Farm
       D   St George's Hill Track
       E   Bathampton Tank
       F   Rifle Range
       G   Site of Duel
       H   Devil's Table
       I   Elsie Luke Cave
       J   Auxiliaries Cave

Fig. 2a View from Bathampton Down looking north-east. A section of the bridleway in the foreground, Bathford and Brown's Folly in the distance, c1935. (R Dyer Collection)

Fig. 2b View from Bathampton Down looking north. Bathampton village in the foreground, Batheaston centre right, c1935. (R Dyer Collection)

THE DOWN DIVIDED

Fig. 3 A section of wall rebuilt in 2008-09.
Looking north with Hampton Down in the foreground
and Hampton Warren beyond the wall. (M F Clark, 2013)

Originally built by Charles Holder in 1718 to enclose his rabbit warren, the wall effectively divided the Down in two. By the late 19th century it had fallen into disuse and a large part had been demolished. This picture shows a section, running along the top of the Iron Age embankment, which has been rebuilt by the Bath Golf Club to separate their practise ground from the main course.

CHARLES HOLDER'S WALL

Until the early 18th century all of the hilltop south of Bathampton village was known as Hampton, or Bath-Hampton, Down but in 1718 this changed when the Lord of the Manor, Charles Holder, ordered a stone wall to be built to divide it in two. His reason for doing so was probably to enclose his rabbit warren but may have been to settle land disputes or to separate his sheep from those belonging to village landholders who had Right of Common (right to pen sheep) on the Down.

The building of the wall caused a good deal of local controversy and resentment, part of which was a long running battle between Bathampton farmer James Charmbury and the Lord of the Manor. Charmbury claimed he had Right of Common to freely pasture sheep on part of the Down and in 1734 Holder, whose family delighted in litigation, took him to court to dispute this.[1] In his defence Charmbury mentioned the new wall and stated that one half of the Down was now called the Farm or Manor Down; as this was part of the Manor and used by Holder, he agreed it had no Common Rights. However he claimed the other half, now called the Parish Down, although also part of the Manor, did have Common Rights. He said it had been open but was now enclosed and included six fields, where the Commoners were allowed to put their sheep when the land was not ploughed and corn not growing. Holder insisted that the farmers should be paying rent for this privilege and won his case.

The wall ran across the Down, from north to south, for just over half a mile. The amount of stone needed to build it must have been considerable and was probably sourced from nearby quarries in the area of the north-eastern promontory. At the time it was built the Down was an open area, devoid of trees, the short turf grazed by sheep and rabbits. The new wall, built of the local Bath Stone, would have stood out like a bright, white ribbon snaking across the grass. The following contemporary illustration shows some of the bare hill tops that surrounded the City – the western slope of Bathampton Down can be seen to the right.

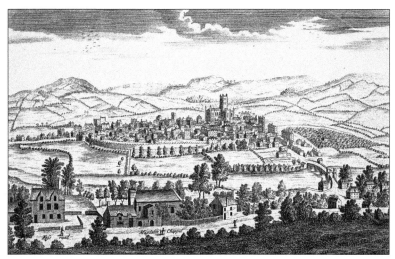

Fig. 4 W Stukeley's View of Bath of 1723 – from the top of the Southern Hill. (© Bath in Time)

The hilltop to the east of the wall became commonly known as Hampton Down and that to the west as Hampton Warren – names which are still sometimes used today. It is not possible to be certain which of these was the Manor Down and which the Parish Down or to ascertain where the six fields were.

The wall can be seen on Thorpe's Map of 1742 and in more detail on *A Survey of the Manours of Hampton, Claverton with Widcombe belonging to Ralph Allen* (from now on referred to as Ralph Allen's Estate Map c1740-64).

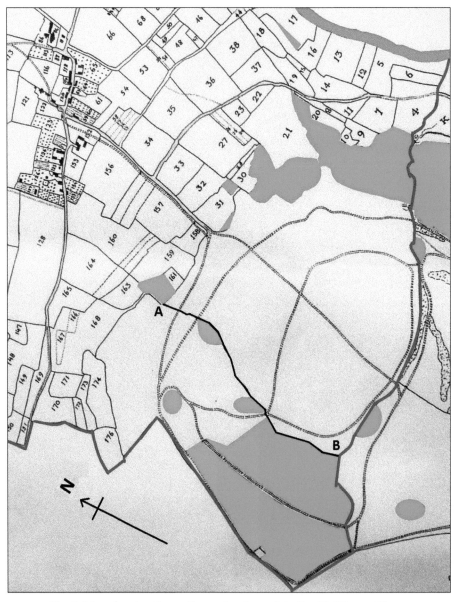

Fig. 5 Map showing the wall running from A to B with Warren House amongst the trees, bottom centre. The dotted lines show Allen's rides. (Based on an adaptation of the Ralph Allen Estate Map, © Mike Chapman, 2007)[2]

This shows the northern end beginning at the top of what is today the right of way or track from St George's Hill up to the Down. The wall then climbs on up to the plateau where it joins the line of the bank and ditch of the Iron Age enclosure, following it southwards until it ends at the Parish Boundary Wall. Three of Allen's fir plantations abut its western side. Two are small but the one at the far end covers a large area and has the Warren House overlooking Bath at its western edge. Three of the rides which Allen used for his own enjoyment and to entertain his guests can be seen intersecting the wall. The Schedule to the Estate Map makes it clear that Ralph Allen now owned the whole area – both Hampton Down and The Warren.

The Bathampton Tithe Map also shows the wall (marked A – B) as seen below :

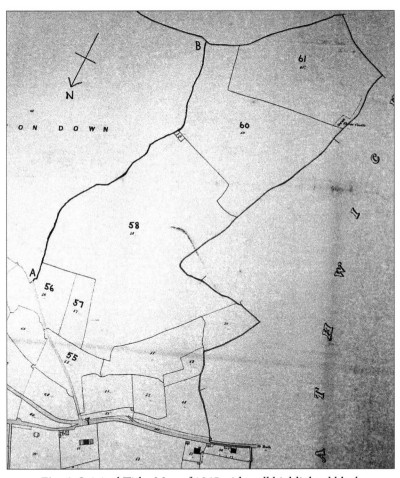

Fig. 6 Original Tithe Map of 1845 with wall highlighted black.
(Somerset Heritage Centre)

Its Apportionment of 1845 shows that east of the wall are 145 acres of open downland which is let to tenant farmers; half of this is now owned by George Edward Allen, Lord of the Manor, and half jointly owned by James Charmbury and George Vivian of Claverton. No. 55, Fussells Wood, has been planted on either side of the St George's Hill Track; above

13

this wood are Nos. 56 and 57, two copses abutting the west side of the wall. The downland on that side, also let to tenant farmers, is owned by Allen and has been divided into two large pastures – No. 58, Hampton Warren Pen, (50 acres) and No. 60, Hampton Warren, (27 acres). The two small fir plantations have gone but a portion of the large one remains as part of an enclosure of 24 acres numbered 61, Fir Grove. This also contains pasture and Sham Castle which has replaced the Warren House.

The large scale Ordnance Survey map of 1888 shows the wall still in place but there are some changes. The Wood, although still known locally as Fussells, is called Pussells by the Ordnance Survey and a rifle range runs west to east on a level area below the northern edge of the high plateau, with the butts in front of the old quarries at its eastern end. The western end is in the Warren which meant that those shooting from the 500 and 600 yard markers had to fire across the wall.

In 1881 the Bath Golf Club opened a nine hole course on Hampton Warren (excluding the area used by the rifle range). In 1893-94 they rented the Hampton Down area so that they could extend the course to eighteen holes 'on the other side of the wall which forms the present boundary'. The wall proved too much of a hazard for golfers playing the then 3rd, 4th, 5th and 7th holes and by the mid-1930s the Club had demolished that part of it.[3] Today little of this historic wall remains. At its northern end it can still be seen in a ruinous state running south across a field up towards the golf course.

Fig. 7 The wall in the field below the golf course with Fussells Wood to the north.
(M F Clark, 2011)

There is no sign of it on the lower part of the course but a few stones survive where it climbs the steep slope to reach the high plateau. In 2008-09 the Golf Club rebuilt a long section from this point, following the line of the Iron Age enclosure to form a boundary for their practise ground. After this it disappears again until just before its southern end where, in 2013, a short stretch of original wall could still be seen near the 16th fairway, standing about four feet high on top of the Iron Age bank. The rebuilding of this section was completed in 2016 by Golf Club Members Thomas and Deborah Bunn.

Fig. 8 Section of the wall re-built 2008-09. (M F Clark, 2009)

Fig. 9 Remains of the old wall at its southern end, with the
Iron Age bank and ditch. (M F Clark, 2013)

PART ONE

The Western Side of the Wall -

HAMPTON WARREN

Fig. 10 From Harvey Wood's *Panoramic View of Bath from Beechen Cliff* c1824.
(© Bath in Time)

The Western side of the Warren runs along the nearest skyline edged by the parish boundary wall; Sham Castle sits on the line of the wall to the far right. The road from Bath to Bathampton is shown between St Mary's Church, Bathwick and the hillside, before disappearing behind the slope of the Down. New houses are being developed in Bathwick and on Bathwick Hill to the right.

HAMPTON WARREN

It is thought that rabbits, or coneys as they were then called, were first successfully established in this country by the Normans. Having been used to warmer weather they needed protection from our cold, damp climate so had to be accommodated in warrens where they were provided with food in winter, shelter, and protection from predators.

Hampton Warren probably dates from about 1256 when the Bishop of Bath and Wells was granted the '*right of free warren*' by Henry II, entitling him to keep rabbits and game in the parishes of Bathampton and Claverton. Built on the western end of Bathampton Down, an isolated hilltop, among the Bronze and Iron Age earthworks, its site is typical of those where warrens were constructed. Similar large warrens were often sited on common land as manorial lords could, by law, keep rabbits on waste areas without infringing the common rights of their tenants. This may lend weight to the supposition that Bathampton farmers possessed common rights on the Warren.

The thin light soil on hilltops was unsuitable for growing crops but provided the good drainage and dry conditions needed for rabbits to thrive. To house them pre-existing earthworks were often utilised and Pillow Mounds were constructed; these were usually rectangular, less than a metre high, ten to thirty metres long and five to twenty metres wide. They were flat on top, had a surrounding ditch and contained stones and man-made tunnels to encourage the rabbits to burrow. At least eleven of these mounds were built on Hampton Warren, some of which can still be seen. They are difficult to identify being easily confused with the remains of ancient field boundaries and the lay-out of the present golf course but two can be recognised fairly easily: a small example fifty metres in front of the seventh tee and the largest, a very long mound which runs along the back of the first green. Typically it is built on a slope at right angles to the contours to assist drainage.

Fig. 11 A small pillow mound can be seen just left of centre, behind the sixth green. (M F Clark, 2013)

Pillow mounds made it easy to capture the rabbits when they were harvested between October and February. Long nets (hays) were set up between them and their feeding grounds, trapping them as they came out at night; alternatively ferrets were put into the burrows on one side and the rabbits caught in purse nets as they bolted out of the exit holes on the other. During the 13th century rabbits were luxury items, prized for their meat and skins – one could cost more than a man's daily wage. Black fur was especially desirable as it was used to trim expensive garments.

In the Middle Ages warrens were administered as part of the manorial estate but from the 15th century they were often leased to a professional Warrener who paid the rent in rabbits. By the 17th and 18th centuries the number of rabbits had increased greatly, they began to stray onto farmland and it became necessary, as at Bathampton, to enclose warrens with dry-stone walling. This kept the rabbits in and helped to deter predators such as rats, stoats and weasels. It also formed a legal boundary – useful when poachers were prosecuted.

Part of the Warrener's job was to trap both rabbits and predators. Pit traps were often constructed in the boundary walls for this purpose. A small square hole made at the base of the wall led into a wooden box tunnel with a drop into a pit at the end. This was covered with a lid, part of which could be lifted to remove the ensnared animals. At Bathampton in a section of the enclosing wall, which now divides the Golf Course from the driving range above Sham Castle, two such holes can be seen. Alternatively they could be the remains of tunnels for hares used when Coursing took place on the Down.

Fig. 12 Example of a pit trap or hare hole. (M F Clark, 2014)

It is likely that Hampton Warren was run on a commercial scale as it was large and had a Warren House or Lodge at its western end where Sham Castle now stands. Such Lodges often occupied similarly isolated, prominent positions enabling the Warrener to protect the stock from poachers. Usually basic longhouses, but sometimes large and ornate, they had a secondary use as hunting lodges, provided a home for the Warrener, and had rooms for drying the skins, storage of carcasses, nets, traps, and tools used to maintain the Pillow Mounds. Very few of these houses remain today.

The first documentary evidence for the Warren House at Bathampton is on a map of the Manor of Bathwick dated 1727.[1] Although it is not in that parish, it is shown just outside its northern boundary. The rectangular building, called 'Anstey's Lodge', appears to have an orchard in front which abuts the parish boundary wall. The area behind the house is annotated 'Hampton Warren'.

Fig. 13 Extract from William Pulteney's Map of Bathwick dated 1727 showing Anstey's Lodge. (© British Library Board)

John Anstey was a Bath Poulterer. In 1732 some rabbits were stolen from his Warren in Bathampton by Henry Broome of Bath, who hid *'five couple of grey rabbits and three couple of black, all upon a stick'* in his cellar – these he sold to George Gale, also a Bath Poulterer, for ten shillings and four pence. When Anstey later bought four of the rabbits from Gale he recognised one of the black ones as his own – he had marked it with a hole punched in the right ear.

The following year he had more problems with poachers. Nathaniel Savery, Labourer of Bath, was accused of unlawfully hunting and killing rabbits belonging to John Anstey, Warrener, having *'frequently used dogs about his Warren'*. When Savery was examined by the justices he stated that he had been with John Harris, Hair Gatherer, when they met George Truman of Widcombe, Keeper of the Warren. Harris, he said, had spat in Truman's face and threatened to kill him. Savery then heard Harris and Broom, a Bath Shoemaker, offer another man, David Hipstone, a bribe of five shillings to take the blame for robbing the Warren. On hearing this Savery *'resolved to make oath of it'*.

When Hipstone, a Broadweaver of Frome, was examined he said that on several occasions during the past year, at night, he saw four Bath men, Harris, Henry and John Broome and Matthew Veale, break into Anstey's Warren. They stole several couple of rabbits out of nets which were pitched there by the Warrener.

One wonders what a Frome weaver was doing at night on Hampton Warren. Possibly he was one of the poachers, unless he was cutting across the Down on his way to or from Bath – the New Warminster Road did not yet exist. It would also be interesting to know the results of the court cases but unfortunately the Quarter Sessions Records only report the examinations of the witnesses, not the outcome.[2]

During the 18th and 19th centuries rabbits had become so plentiful that the price fell. Better meat was available for those who could afford it – rabbit stew became a staple food for the poor. The fur was now used to make cheap hats. As a result Warrens declined and closed – this seems to have been the case at Bathampton.

Richard Jones (Ralph Allen's Clerk of Works) hints at the closure of the Warren in his memoirs. He states that Allen bought the Bathampton Estate in about 1742, and then '*began to plant the Warren, which was a rabbit warren before*'. He put in groups of fir trees and a large plantation known as Fir Forest which surrounded the Warren House on three sides.[3] This can be seen on Ralph Allen's Estate Map, c1740-64, which, although it has a picture of Sham Castle (built 1762) on its border, still shows the Warren House among the trees – a long rectangular building, with two rooms, facing west as seen below.

Fig. 14 Warren House shown on Ralph Allen's Estate Map, c1740-64.
Two of his rides can also be seen marked in pink. (Bath Record Office)

There are many pictures of Sham Castle, but only one image showing Warren House has been found. It is depicted in a drawing of North Parade, Bath by Letitia Bush c1740; the house can just be seen in the background, standing alone on the empty hilltop overlooking the City. It appears large, and is a long, one story building with a two story porch at the front. The date is probably correct as it is not yet surrounded by Fir Forest.

Fig. 15 Close-up of Warren House – from a drawing of North Parade, Bath by Letitia Bush c1740.
(© No 1 Royal Crescent, Bath Preservation Trust)

In 1748 the old house was the scene of a violent murder (see pages 25 to 28). The building was demolished shortly afterwards and Sham Castle built on the site in 1762. The days of the commercial Warren at Bathampton were over but rabbits continued to be caught there for many years afterwards.

The *Bath Chronicle* carries a number of reports showing that poaching was still rife on Hampton Warren and Hampton Down. On 26 May 1780, '*game upon the Manor of Bathampton has of late been much destroyed*' and all '*unqualified persons*' found trespassing '*will be prosecuted with the utmost severity*'. This warning was clearly not heeded as on 9 August 1781, '*game on the Manors of Claverton and Bathampton has been almost totally destroyed by poachers*' and '*the Hazel Woods thereon have been shamefully damaged by people in the Nutting Seasons*'.

Problems continued throughout the following century. A report on 1 January 1852 excited considerable interest as it involved two local Magistrates. One was F T Allen Esq., of Grosvenor House, Bath, who was summoned for trespassing '*in pursuit of rabbits*' on lands tenanted by the other, P C Sheppard of the Manor House, Bathampton. Sheppard's brother had met Allen and his servant Isaac Bence '*near Ham Wood*' – they were carrying a gun, a net with a live rabbit in it and a bag containing ferrets. He immediately charged them with trespassing and '*an altercation ensued*' in which each gentleman called the other a liar and the enraged Mr Sheppard threatened to strike Allen on the head with his gun. Allen told the court that he had been allowed to shoot on the estate by the late Lord of the Manor; the Magistrate, although unwilling to convict a colleague, considered the case proved and fined him 40 shillings.

Six years later the paper of 2 September 1858 reported that William Wheeler, gentleman of Bath, had been summoned by Thomas Newth, gamekeeper for Mr Wilson of Claverton Manor, for trespass and shooting two partridges in Sham Castle Field. Mr John Ruddick, who lived in nearby Sham Castle Cottage, claimed to have seen the incident but had reason to dislike Wheeler as he had just dismissed his son and had refused Ruddick permission to serve teas to picnickers on a piece of land which he owned adjoining Ruddick's cottage. On the day in question Newth had arranged to meet Wheeler at Hampton Rocks to shoot rabbits. As he could not get any ferrets he did not turn up so Wheeler and his friend James Lane returned home. On their way they passed through the Warren (where Wheeler had authority to shoot) and got over a wall into the beech copse at the top of Sham Castle Field to inspect some wood. Oats were growing in the field and Lane, on seeing a rabbit, ran towards it but came straight back. Wilson then fired both barrels of his gun into the Warren to clear out the powder. His solicitor closed the defence by stating that both Wheeler and Lane were highly respected men, unlikely to flout the gun laws. The magistrate said the evidence was very contradictory but gave Wheeler the benefit of the doubt. He thought that Lane had gone on the land to get at a rabbit, but not wilfully, so fined him one shilling for trespass.

Another man who went ferreting at Hampton Rocks was William Bishop, whose case came up on 12 October 1867. Bull, assistant gamekeeper to Major Ralph Shuttleworth Allen of Bathampton Manor, had caught him there with some nets, a ferret and a brown terrier. Bishop claimed that he had a right to be there as it was a public thoroughfare but Major Allen said that *'there was no right of way there whatever, he only allowed the public to use it'* and in any case Bishop had been caught there before.

Bishop was fined ten shillings or a week in prison, but asked for a reduction as he had only one leg. This excuse did not gain the Magistrates sympathy and he was told sharply to pay up or his fine would be doubled.[4]

Doubtless poaching continued after this, particularly during the war years when meat was in very short supply. Rabbits were almost eradicated when the disease myxomatosis spread to this country from the continent in 1953. As a result the last commercial rabbit warren in England closed in 1954. Over the years the rabbits have returned and can now be found once more on Hampton Warren.

Fig. 16 Cross-section of a rabbit warren.
(Google Images: Boston University School of Education)

MURDER AT
THE WARREN HOUSE

The last occupants of the Warren House were Richard Biggs and his family. Originally a baker by trade, he had recently turned his hand to what is described as husbandry – presumably he was the Warrener. During June 1748 Biggs and his wife Ruth went to visit the Spring Gardens – popular pleasure grounds at Bathwick which were on the site of the present Bath Recreation Ground. While they were there Ruth Biggs lost her garter and it was found by an unsuccessful suitor for her hand who, as a joke, flaunted it *before the eyes of her husband*. He became suspicious and on their return home a quarrel ensued. The infuriated and jealous Biggs would not listen to her explanation and beat his wife to death *in a cruel and barbarous manner* then carried her body on his back down to the River Avon and threw it in.

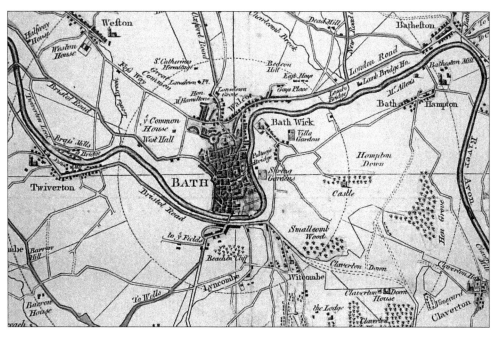

Fig. 17 From *Taylor & Meyler's Map of Five Miles around Bath*, 1787.
(Bath Record Office)

On the morning of Wednesday 15 June the corpse was found in the river at Dolemead in the parish of Lyncombe and Widcombe. She had been shockingly beaten *her head, breast, arms and thighs were covered in bruises and wounds, her lower parts were greatly swelled and black*. At the inquest held that day the Coroner noted that her husband had absconded on Tuesday and brought in a verdict of wilful murder against him. She was buried in the churchyard at St Thomas à Becket, Widcombe, on Friday 17.[1] As the body had been found in Lyncombe and Widcombe the Parish Officers there were not only responsible for the burial but also for bringing the murderer to justice. They offered a reward of 2 guineas for

Biggs' capture and issued the following description: '*5ft 6ins tall, dark complexion, round favoured, has a down look, a pretty thick beard, dark hair, aged about 30. He was wearing a blue waistcoat and breeches, trimmed with brass buttons when he went missing*'.

Twelve days later Biggs was captured on 29 June at Rudge near Beckington and was sent to the Bridewell at Shepton Mallett by the local JP. Here he confessed to an argument followed by blows but said his wife died falling into a quarry. He gave '*a trifling reason*' for carrying Ruth's body more than a mile on his back and throwing it into the river.

His trial took place at the Somerset Assizes in Taunton on Tuesday 23 August. The unfortunate ratepayers of Lyncombe and Widcombe again bore the brunt of the costs involved; the Vestry Minutes dated 30 November 1748 record their expenses, '*2 guineas for apprehending Richard Biggs*' and '*£13 15s 9d expended at the Assizes in prosecuting him re: 11 witnesses, counsels' fees, charges of Mr Dodd, Surgeon, and other charges incident thereto*'.[2]

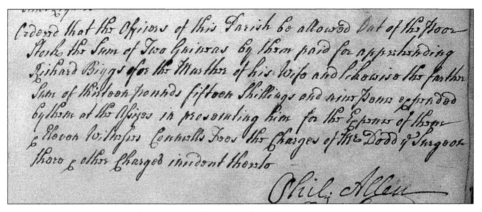

Fig. 18 Entry from Lyncombe & Widcombe Vestry Minutes 1732-54.
(Somerset Heritage Centre)

During the trial many in the courtroom were moved to tears as Biggs' eleven year old son gave the deciding evidence against him. He was found guilty of the murder of his wife and sentenced to be hanged in chains at Odd Down, near Bath.

After the trial the condemned man was imprisoned at Ilchester Gaol and behaved in a very sullen manner while awaiting his execution. He was, however, '*troubled at the thought of being hung in chains, as when the smith came to measure him for his irons he flew into a temper and refused him*'.

Biggs' execution was to take place in Gallows Tyning, a large field (now built over) which occupied the corner between Bloomfield Road and Rush Hill on a hilltop to the south-west of Bath. It was said to be '*in sight of the house where he lived*' – there is still a clear view of Odd Down from the Sham Castle area, where the Warren House once stood.

On the evening of Monday 12 September the prisoner was brought from Ilchester to Bath '*as privately as possible*'. He would have been accompanied by the County Sheriff, the hangman, a priest and an armed escort (to prevent his escape or any public disorder). It was customary to organise stops at local inns along the way, where the condemned man would be given a free drink (this may be the origin of the expression 'one for the road') but owing to the privacy of the journey it is doubtful whether this practice was followed.

Between two and three pm on Wednesday 14, Biggs was brought on horseback to the gibbet on Odd Down. Once again his behaviour throughout was sullen. He spent an hour in prayer with the Rev. Dr. Coney and then mounted one of the ladders and the executioner the other. However, when the hangman tried to put the rope around his neck, he threw himself on the ground and lay there helplessly. It was too difficult to get him up again so the rope was tied to a rung of the ladder and he was put on a horse's back and dragged off from there. Twenty thousand spectators who had come from miles around to see him suffer were disappointed '*as he hung low and could not easily be seen*'.

Biggs' body was hung in chains on the gibbet '*near to the road and appeared a most frightening spectacle, most offensive to wayfarers*'. Three months later, in early January, the body was taken down during the night '*by persons unknown*', who left their ladder near the gibbet. They threw the body into the Avon where it was found, still in irons, when the river was drawn at Twerton on 29 May 1749. Biggs' remains were buried near the Cloth Factory and Brass Mills on Twerton Island (known for many years afterwards as Biggs' Island). The iron gallows cap, surmounted by a hook, survives in the collection of the Bath Royal Literary and Scientific Institute.

Many sightseers from Bath crossed the river via the Spring Gardens Ferry on their way to gaze at the blood spattered scene of the murder. As a result, Ralph Allen, who had bought the Bathampton Estate seven years previously, had the Warren House '*razed to the ground*' shortly after Biggs' burial.

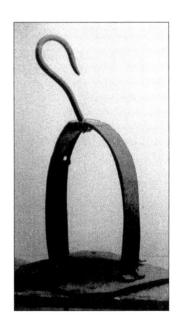

Left :
  Fig. 19 Line drawing of a
  complete 18th century 'cage'
  or set of 'irons'.
  (Google Images; Wikipedia.org)

Right :
  Fig. 20 The original gallows
  cap held by the BRLSI.
  (BLHRG, A H Green Collection)

The following poem appeared in the *Bath Guardian* nearly a hundred years later. Although full of inaccuracies it shows that the unfortunate episode had not been forgotten.

SHAM CASTLE AND ITS LEGEND
by Tom True

1
In days of yore, on yonder hill
A lowly cottage stood -
Near it there was a purling rill,
And at it's back a wood;
Sylvan retreat! Enchanted spot!
Why dwelt not love within that cot!

2
There beauty lived, but fate decreed
She should unhappy be,
Youth was condemned with age to lead
A life of misery.
How vain to think that Autumn's blight
In genial Spring can take delight.

3
Her husband who had never loved,
Love's power could never feel;
His icy heart her woes unmoved,
Could see, nor strive to heal,
Although full well he knew 'twas he
Who caused them by his jealousy.

4
Her love was lavished on her boy,
A prattling infant he,
Who was his mother's only joy,
And shared her sympathy;
When wandering through the woods alone,
She track'd his steps and led him home.

5
One win'try eve when snow fell fast,
She had retired to rest,
Forgiveness of her Maker ask'd,
And her sweet boy had bless'd,
Unsullied, free from guilty fear,
Oh! How serene her slumbers were.

6
At midnight hour as he returned
From drunken revelry,
His heated brain then maddening burn'd,
With green-eyed jealousy;
In frenzied rage he seized a knife,
And with it stabbed his sleeping wife.

7
Without a groan but one soft sigh,
Thus in her sleep she died;
That brutal man her bleeding corpse
Dragg'd to the river side,
And plung'd it in before his son,
Who wildly through the snow had run.

8
But scarce was o'er this deed of blood
'Ere Justice did pursue,
And he where once his cottage stood
Was hung exposed to view -
And on his carcase birds might feed;
(His child divulged the wicked deed).

Fig. 21 A late 18th century execution. (Source Unknown)

A TIME OF CHANGE
- the impact of Ralph Allen

Ralph Allen had amassed a considerable fortune from his business enterprises by the mid 18th Century, this enabled him to build Prior Park, a mansion overlooking Bath, with landscaped gardens running northwards down the hillside towards the City. It also had a considerable area of adjoining land on Claverton Down which once belonged to the Priors of Bath Abbey and was used for hunting. Allen moved into his new home in December 1741 and was able to enlarge his estate further when he purchased Bathampton Manor in 1743 and Claverton Manor in 1758. These, together with Prior Park, formed a single large and scenic tract of land to the south-east of Bath, ideal for a rich man to develop and use for entertaining his many important guests. After he became Lord of Bathampton Manor he made changes which enhanced Hampton Warren and Hampton Down by planting fir trees, creating rides and building a folly.

These are all shown on his Estate Map.[1] Although undated it is believed to have been gradually compiled in the years between 1740 and Allen's death in 1764 as it has numerous features relating to dates within these years and includes the Bathampton Manor and Claverton Manor Estates.

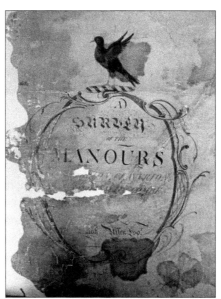

Fig. 22 The Cornish Chough, Ralph Allen's crest, surmounts
the title shield on his Estate Map. (Bath Record Office)

The Fir Plantations

It is thought that Ralph Allen planted more than 55,000 fir trees on his lands, in time these would not only enhance the landscape but also provide a cash crop of pine boarding which could be sold to the builders of Bath. By 1743 land on Hampton Warren was no longer needed for the 'farming' of rabbits. Instead the first of Allen's plantations was established at its western end, covering what is now Sham Castle Field and extending north-eastwards almost as far as the present television masts. This was known as 'Fir Forest' or 'Fir Grove' and was by far the largest such plantation on the hilltop. Other much smaller groups were planted on both the Down and the Warren providing points of interest on the otherwise bare downland. The plantations proved a temptation for thieves. On 1 February 1752 the *Bath Journal* reported that Shaderick Cooper, '*a well-set man with a dark brown complexion*', had been arrested for stealing several fir trees from Hampton Warren but had escaped from custody. A ten pound reward was offered for his capture. The trees began to be felled in the 1790s, well after Ralph Allen's death.

Ralph Allen's Rides

Ralph Allen's Clerk of Works, Richard Jones, recorded that his employer created ten or twelve miles of carriage rides over his estates.[2] These radiate out from Prior Park, Allen's mansion house at Widcombe, and criss-cross Hampton Down; Hampton Warren; Claverton Down and the Prior's Park, linking with the manor houses of Hampton and Claverton. Allen took great pleasure in taking his many prominent visitors on outings to admire his estates and the extensive, unobscured scenery that could be enjoyed from the Downs.

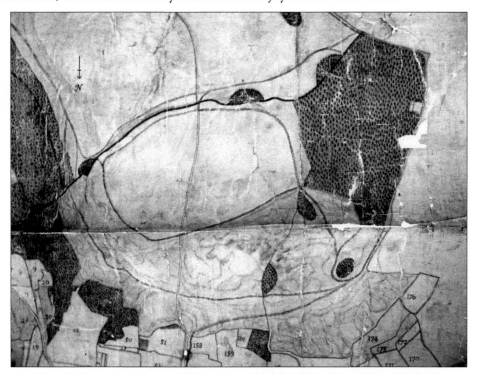

Fig. 23 Hampton Down and Warren from Ralph Allen's Estate Map, c1740-64.
The southern parish boundary is the black line running centre left to top right.
The rides are pink. 'Downs Lane' as it leaves the Down is at the bottom
between fields 51 and 158 with the ride to the Manor House on its western edge.
(See also Figs. 14 and 25) (Bath Record Office)

When Lady Luxborough visited Allen in 1752[3] he showed her the beautiful surroundings by driving her through a ride of 14 or 15 miles '*and they stopped at many points to gain lovely views of the City, the river and the country around. So varied were the prospects that her Ladyship was enchanted*' and '*the open down, where the scene was sufficiently wild and picturesque pleased Lady Luxborough's fancy*'.

One of the rides entered the parish of Hampton from the south-west (top right of previous map; see also Fig. 14) at the edge of Allen's largest fir plantation and followed the parish boundary wall as it ran northwards. Here he built the wall with both rough and large cut blocks of stone which gave a pleasant 'semi formal' foreground to the wide vista that could be enjoyed from this point – not only of the City of Bath but beyond to the Mendip Hills, Avon Gorge and south-western flanks of the Cotswold Hills. Today the wall is mostly in a sad state of repair, but sections showing the use of both rough and cut stone can still be seen. Similar work can be found at the top of Widcombe Hill – in a wall on the south side of the road – which no doubt also formed part of the rides.

Fig. 24 Section of wall showing the rough and cut blocks of stone used by Ralph Allen.
(G M Huggins, 2014)

The network over Hampton Down included a circuit of the Iron Age Enclosure (shown centre of Fig. 23) – the mound and ditch of which must have aroused much interest, as did the folly of Sham Castle after it was built in 1762.

Many of today's public footpaths over the Down closely follow the routes that were laid out by Allen. However, instead of using the ancient rough and sunken 'Downs Lane' [part of which forms today's bridleway] that led from the Down to Hampton village he created a parallel route passing down through fields to the west of the lane. At the bottom of the hill it continued across the meadows to the Manor House – thus avoiding the few properties that then made up the village.

Much of this ride has now been built on, but it is possible to see a small section in the upper part of the field known as Great Lye – numbered 158 on the map. Ralph Allen's gateway leading from the Down into the field can still be traced, but the original stone gate posts, with their guard stones, are now hidden within the hedge line. From time to time this opening has been reinstated in order to give cattle grazing on the Down access to lower pastures.

Fig. 25 Extract from Ralph Allen's Estate Map looking south.
The ride leading from Hampton Down to Hampton Manor is shown
in pink running down parallel to the 'Downs Lane' and across
the meadows to the Manor House. (Bath Record Office)

Fig. 26 The western post and guard stone of the gateway on the ride leading from Hampton Down to Hampton Manor. (G M Huggins, 2014)

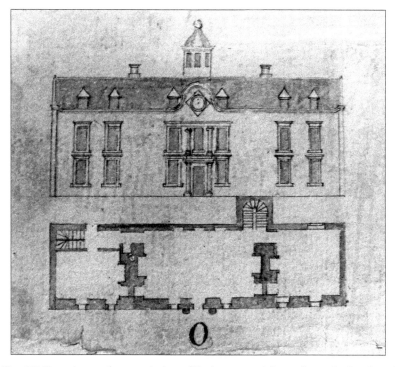

Fig. 27 Drawing and ground plan of Bathampton Manor from the border of Ralph Allen's Estate Map, c1740-64. (Bath Record Office)

No further evidence of these rides on the Down appears to have survived.

Sham Castle

During the eighteenth century it became fashionable for the wealthy to ornament their estates with temples, grottoes and follies. Ralph Allen was no exception and after landscaping his garden at Prior Park was persuaded to build a folly on Bathampton Down. In 1755 William Pitt, politician, enthusiastic gardener and one of Allen's circle of eminent friends, wrote to Sanderson Miller the gentleman architect and landscape designer, asking him to draw up plans for *'a considerable Gothic Object which is to stand in a very fine situation on the hills near Bath'.*[4] These plans do not survive but may have been for a building referred to by Richard Jones. He states that plans were drawn up for his master to build a *'long pile at the point of the hill, facing the London Road and Hampton'* but he *'put him off that which would have cost £250'.*

The site eventually chosen was the clearing in the Fir Grove, on the edge of Hampton Warren overlooking the City of Bath, where the Warren House had recently been demolished. According to Jones he drew up the plans for *'the Castle in the Warren'*, began work on it in 1762 and finished it in a *'quarter of a year'.* He *'would have built it larger, for an object to be seen further off, but was hindered by my master and other gentlemen'.*

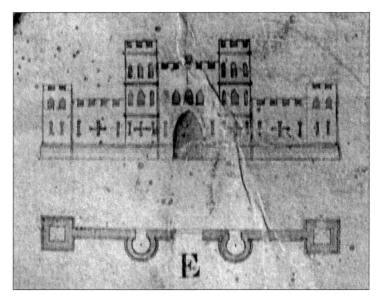

Fig. 28 Drawing and ground plan of Sham Castle a later addition to the
border of Ralph Allen's Estate Map c1740-64. (Bath Record Office)

The Castle, built of coursed squared rubble with a decorative band of large, rough, vermiculated stones at the base, (see Fig. 31) is in fact purely a frontage with nothing behind and has a central arch with semi-circular towers on each side; these are adjoined by short walls each of which ends in a square tower. The whole façade is battlemented and has blind lancet windows and arrow loops, which are typical of Sanderson Miller's work. If Jones' claim is correct perhaps he simply produced a smaller and cheaper version of Miller's plan. The Castle had been designed as an *'eye catcher'* to improve the view from Allen's Bath town house which was to the rear of North Parade Passage. It could not be seen from his home at Prior Park but, like that mansion, provided a good advertisement for the Bath Stone produced at his quarries. Those travelling to Bath down the old road from Lansdown had an excellent view of it silhouetted against the fir trees on the opposite hilltop. It soon became known as Sham Castle, probably as it was not real but perhaps because a stretch of nearby hillside in Bathwick was known as The Sham Down long before the Castle was erected.[5]

An early description was given in 1781 by Edmund Rack: '*On the north-west brow fronting the City, is a noble plantation of Scotch and Spruce firs, in the foreground of which and immediately under them is a pretty fictitious castle, the deception is a very pleasing one, the light colour of the stone forming a fine contrast with the deep mass of shade formed by the plantations close behind it. This building and plantation appear beautiful objects not only from almost every part of the City, but through a great extent of country westwards*'.[6]

Fig. 29 Sham Castle from North Parade Bridge, c1850. (© Bath in Time)

The Castle's surroundings were a popular venue for all kinds of sports and celebrations from the time it was built and possibly before when the Warren House occupied the site. On 12 June 1766 the *Chronicle* printed a stern warning from Clutterbuck, the Bathampton Estate's Solicitor: '*It has become a custom for idle people to assemble at the Castle in the Fir Grove, coming there in a disorderly manner, to play at fives. The public are given notice that any future trespassers will be prosecuted with the utmost severity*'. Presumably they had been playing hand-ball against the Castle wall.

Almost fifty years later the *Bath Journal* reports that a subscription fête was held on Claverton Down on 6 July 1814 to celebrate the signing of the Peace Treaty with France. It was attended by thousands of people and refreshments consisted of '*four oxen (one roasted whole and two in quarters on the Down, and one baked whole in the City and sent up to the spot), eight sheep, 400 dozen penny loaves and twenty butts of strong beer*'. The *Journal*, however, complained that there was not enough to go around but was happy to say that '*no material accident occurred upon this memorable occasion*'. In the evening a large bonfire in the shape of a pyramid, was built in an '*elevated situation*' and was seen from all parts of the City when it '*blazed in a most tremendous column of flame*'. Sham Castle was illuminated '*in a most attractive and brilliant style*' but unfortunately the fireworks did not arrive in time and were let off from Beechen Cliff the following evening. A printing press was set up on the Down especially for the occasion and ran off the following souvenir poem.[7]

ADDRESS IN COMMEMORATION OF PEACE
between Russia, Austria, Prussia, Sweden, France and England
Printed by GYE and SON, of the Market Place, Bath.
At the Wellington Press, in the centre of Claverton Down, near Bath,
on Wednesday, 6 July 1814.

All the Parishes appear,
Come to hail the PARISH here
PEACE, with PARISH in her train,
Comes to bless old BLADUD'S plain

See the feasts they now prepare,
Hark, the shouts that rend the air!
See the bill directs the way,
To the sports prepar'd to-day:
This day, by British valour won -
Led by godlike WELLINGTON!

All the laurels we have won -
All the good your ZEAL has done -
See the PRINTERS too appear
On the spot recording here!
Now's the time to tell your SON
The triumphs You for him have won -
TAKE IT, place it in his hand -
That HE, like YOU, may prove a blessing
to the LAND!

W.H.P.

The heading states that it was printed on Claverton Down, however the whole of the hilltop, although divided between the parishes of Bathampton and Claverton, was often referred to locally as Claverton Down. Sham Castle is actually on the Hampton Warren area of Bathampton Down.

An undated poster[8] (collected by John Weeks, famous landlord of the Bush Tavern in central Bristol), advertises rural sports to take place on the Down '*during the afternoon*'. These included a donkey race, sack and running races, mock cock fights and various competitions such as apple bobbing, the first to eat a quart of hasty pudding, diving in a pail of flour for a lead bullet and last but not least a pig hunt, the winner to keep the pig. All these were interspersed with music and the whole event was to conclude with '*a magnificent bonfire, flights of rockets and Roman Candles and a brilliant illumination of the Sham Castle*'. It also refers to the peace celebrations of 1814 which were somewhat premature as Napoleon escaped from Elba and the conflict was not finally settled until the Battle of Waterloo the following year.

In 1816 another poster[9] advertised a Bull Bait which was to take place in the afternoon of 4 May on Claverton Down, directly behind Sham Castle. A fine young bull was to be baited by English Bull Dogs followed immediately afterwards by a Badger Bait, with a variety of other sports. Refreshments of every description were to be available for the company assembled on the Down.

This was not the only violent form of entertainment to take place. The *Chronicle* of 28 January 1864 reported that Joseph Orchard of Bath and Thomas Flower of Radstock were summoned for fighting on the Down. Police Sergeant Chant had found a large crowd of rough people, many from Bristol, assembled there and the defendants stripped off and fighting. There was all the appearance of a prize fight and when a gentleman on horseback shouted '*police*' the two boxers hastily dressed and walked away, pretending that they had merely squabbled in Bath and were settling their differences. The officer, however, told the court that they were fighting for £2 and that one of their seconds was the ex-champion of Australia. The two boxers got off lightly with a requirement to find sureties for their good behaviour for six months.

By 1867 the old Castle had '*been in a state of decay for many years*' and Major Ralph Shuttleworth Allen, of Bathampton Manor, intended having it restored.

Fig. 30 The 'Sham Castle' showing how it had started to decay. Engraving from *Rambles Around Bath*, 2nd edition, 1848, by James Tunstall. (Google Books)

It seems he deferred the repairs as on 29 April 1880 the *Chronicle* reported the Castle was being renovated. The square side towers had been falling to pieces stone by stone, most of the damage having been done by boys using the area for their games. Major Allen was having the upper portions of these towers rebuilt and the centre circular towers restored so that the Castle would soon be almost as good as new. Close inspection of the stonework today reveals evidence of these repairs and further alterations to prevent vandalism.

In June 1892 the paper reported fighting of a more serious kind after the 1st Volunteer Battalion of the Somerset Light Infantry marched from Bath to Claverton for a Field Day on the 11th. Part detached at North Road to form the defending force, the remainder went on to form up on ground near Claverton Manor. From here they began their attack, advanced in search of the enemy, opened fire when they were found '*well posted behind the boundary wall of Bathampton Down*' and drove their opponents back to Sham Castle where they were defeated. Cease fire sounded, the Battalion '*marched past*' and refreshments were served before the men marched back to the City.

Five years later Bath celebrated Queen Victoria's Silver Jubilee in style with, amongst other things, the opening of Henrietta Park, a procession of seven thousand children, church services, treats for young and old and of course, fireworks at Sham Castle. For almost an hour rockets of various kinds were sent up in quick succession, the building itself being outlined with fifteen hundred fairy lights. (Also called candle lamps these were small thick glass jars, often coloured, containing a lit candle and suspended by a wire handle fixed around the rim).

Afterwards a tragedy almost occurred when the spectators left after the fireworks. They all hurried down the steep slope towards the North Road, those in front could not get through the gate onto the road quickly enough and the mass of people soon became closely packed, with pressure increasing on those nearest the narrow wicket gate. Luckily several gentlemen prevented a tragedy when they managed to keep it open and pull people through, the only casualty being a young woman who fainted but was revived by water from the cottages below the Castle.

After the First World War the old way of life changed drastically, many country estates were no longer viable and were split up and sold. This was the case at Bathampton and neighbouring Bathwick – both estates were put up for sale at the same time. The Bathampton Estate, bought by Ralph Allen in 1742, had remained in the Allen family for several generations before being sold by Henry Allen in 1921. Some parts, mainly the farms, were sold privately to sitting tenants and the remainder was auctioned by Messrs Fortt, Hatt and Billings at 3 pm on Wednesday 6 April at the Grand Pump Room Hotel in Bath.

Fig. 31 From the Bathampton Estate Sale Catalogue, April 1921. (Bath Record Office)

The sale catalogue included Lot 17 '*The Castle Field and Sham Castle*' (No. 61 on the Tithe Map). This contained about 24 acres of freehold pasture land with coppice and '*The Historic Sham Castle*' all of which was in the occupation of Bathampton farmer Mr G T Candy. The land was approached from the North Road over a right of way belonging to the Bathwick Estate and held under a yearly agreement. The Lot description finished by suggesting that '*this pleasantly situate plot of land, which commands delightful views over the City and adjoins the Bath Golf Club House forms a delightful position for the erection of private Residences, Bungalows, etc*'.

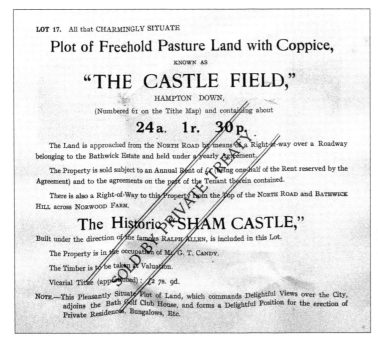

Fig. 32 The catalogue entry for Lot 17. (Bath Record Office)

Lot 17 was sold by private treaty to farmer Candy before the auction. He retained the field but put the Castle up for auction again on 6 June at the Fernley Hotel with Mr Bertram Fortt as the auctioneer. It was hoped that the '*familiar edifice with about an acre of land adjoining*' would always be preserved however its surroundings were developed. It was suggested that the immediate vicinity would make an admirable tea garden considering the number of people who enjoyed '*a jaunt*' to the delightful Down. Other suggestions were a restaurant, boarding house, school and the addition of an asbestos back to the Castle to convert it to a bungalow which could be occupied by golfers during the season.

On 28 May the *Chronicle* published a humorous poem sent in by Mr Ernest Crawford about the forthcoming sale:

'*The Baron of old built a fastness of stone*
And safe in his stronghold, he well held his own;
But modern equipment and new ways of arming
Would oust the old baron and give him a warning.
So come to our auction and have some good sport
In seeing a castle knock'd down by a FORTT'!

Despite Mr Fortt's best efforts the Castle did not sell and on 9 July the *Chronicle* was pleased to announce that it had been purchased privately by two gentlemen for presentation to the City, thankfully ensuring its future *'as a notable landmark of Bath'.* Three weeks later the paper announced that the Corporation had been pleased to accept the gift. The gentlemen, Mr Arthur Edward Withy, a prominent and public spirited citizen, who founded the Bath law firm of Withy, King and Lee and his friend Richard Rusden Ottley, a retired schoolmaster, had the Castle put into good repair and included twenty-five pounds with their gift to erect a fence around the ground on which it stood. In fact it appears that Messrs Withy and Ottley made a donation to the Bath Corporation who then purchased the Castle and approximately an acre of land around it for £175 from George Thomas Candy and George Dickenson Candy on 5 November 1921. The plot measured about 153 feet on the east, 122 feet on the north and 108 feet on the south and west sides.[10]

The kindness and forethought of these two gentlemen was subsequently recorded on a plaque, illustrated on the right, which was placed over the central arch.

Today Sham Castle still stands looking out over Bath. At night it looks beautiful when floodlit, giving the appearance of a castle hanging in the air but it is not so easy to see from the City in daylight because of the surrounding trees.

Fig. 33
(G M Huggins, 2014)

Fig. 34 Sham Castle from the City. (G M Huggins, 2014)

QUEEN'S COLLEGE
- what might have been

The view of Sham Castle on its hilltop would no longer exist had plans to build a large and magnificent Anglican College on the site come to fruition.

During the 1830s concern was growing throughout the country over the rise of the Catholic religion. In 1828 Bishop Baines had purchased Prior Park, Ralph Allen's former mansion in Bath for use as a seminary, and by 1838 nine Catholic Colleges had opened in England, three of which were in Somerset. This appalled a group of Anglicans in Bath, who were strongly opposed to Catholicism and wished to check its progress, particularly in the field of education. They felt that the new colleges were '*an awful warning of approaching evil and spread of that faith at variance with our pure and holy religion*' and decided to provide an alternative educational establishment for their sons, to be built on a site chosen from three around the City.

By November 1838 they had opened an Estate Office at 1 Laura Place where the public could see the drawings and the prospectus for the College, which was to be funded by subscription shares and named Queen's College as a tribute to Queen Victoria and after the Oxford College of that name.

The prospectus stated that the site chosen was '*on one of the heights of the City, called Sham Castle, or Claverton Down*' where '*land had been taken in the Parishes of Bathwick and Bathampton*'. The College, which would be an Auxiliary of Oxford and Cambridge Universities, was to be partly ready for an initial 215 students in eighteen months, the cost of building being estimated at £30,000. It was to include a Junior School and Almshouses for '*twenty four aged persons*' and its main purpose was to '*establish solid principles of Christianity and prove a bulwark against ignorance and superstition*'. The behaviour of the boys was also paramount as, to prevent '*improper conduct, no student would be allowed to walk in Bath or within three miles of the City, without his cap and gown, on pain of rustication*'.

Fig. 35 The architect chosen was James Wilson whose design sketch shows an imposing neo-gothic pile, probably on the level site of Sham Castle. (© Bath in Time)

There were to be Student's Rooms, Lecture Rooms, Tutor's Apartments, a Warden's Lodge and a Chapel. The planned curriculum was extensive including Languages, Mathematics and Sciences, Law, Medicine, Engineering and the Arts. The tutors and the Warden would all be Graduates of Oxford or Cambridge.

On 21 February 1839 the *Bath Chronicle* carried an advertisement for this *'national undertaking'* which would be a *'lucrative investment of capital, of highest interest to parents who desire their sons to have a liberal and profound education'*. The newspaper however did not share this view and published a disclaimer on the same day. It did not wish to be responsible for its readers investing in the project which it felt could be a total failure and anything but beneficial to the established church.

The *Bath and Cheltenham Gazette* included Wilson's drawing of the College in its edition of 25 June that year, describing it as a massive, noble *'but very beautiful edifice which will be seated on the brow of Claverton Down, overlooking Bath, so conspicuous that it can be seen from every part of the City, forming the most prominent feature in the landscape'*.

Advertisements for shareholders continued to be published throughout 1839 and early 1840. The scheme was running into difficulties and a new committee was formed in the hope of bringing the project *'to a prosperous issue'*. It seems that it was not possible to sell enough shares to fund the building of such a grandiose College and on 20 August 1840 a last, somewhat desperate, appeal appeared in the *Bath Chronicle*. This reminded readers that the new, highly respectable, committee guaranteed that the plans would meet with public approval and hoped that the share list would rapidly fill as *'pecuniary means alone are wanting'*.

It appears that a start was made on building the College as in *Rambles About Bath and its Neighbourhood* (1848), James Tunstall describes walking along the edge of the Down past Sham Castle as follows: *'we pass the forsaken terrace of a projected college, now the garden of the cottage just below the Castle'*. This long narrow terrace runs north-south below the Castle on the Bathwick side of the Bathampton/Bathwick parish boundary wall. On its long western side there remains a substantial retaining wall built of blocks of dressed Bath stone.

Fig. 36 The terrace wall from the west with Sham Castle beyond. (M F Clark, 2014)

The Bathwick Tithe Map of 1840 does not show the terrace or wall. The area is part of a large enclosure of Downland Pasture (No. 40), owned and occupied by James Powick and others who were leasing it on behalf of the College. Adjoining this and abutting the North Road is a small wood called Queen's College Plantation, (No. 41), owned and occupied by the Duke of Cleveland. After the project failed the pasture reverted to the Bathwick Estate.

The Tithe Map was probably drawn up earlier than 1840 as the accompanying schedule is dated 1838, before building of the College began in 1839-40. This would account for the wall and terrace not being shown. They are on Cotterell's 1852 *Plan of the City of Bath and its Suburbs*. The terrace is occupied by a market garden (shown hatched) bounded by the parish boundary wall on the east, the College wall on the west and with Sham Castle Cottage, the ruins of which can still be seen, newly constructed at its northern end. The plan also records a further wall, running parallel to the above, but this no longer exists.

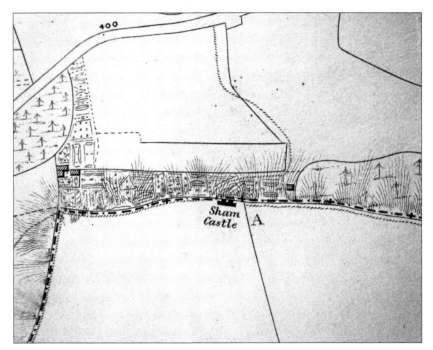

Fig. 37 Extract from Cotterell and Spackman's *Plan of the City of Bath and Suburbs*, 1852-3, looking west. (Bath Record Office)

As the wall can be dated to 1838-52 from the maps it is probable that Tunstall was correct and it was part of the proposed College site. Later the resulting terrace provided an excellent site for the market garden and its attendant cottage.

Had Queen's College been built it would have had a tremendous impact on the Sham Castle area and could have led to the urbanisation of the site, although it is not known how far it would have extended into Bathampton Parish. Thankfully the old Castle was not demolished to make way for the College and the view of it and the surrounding hillside can still be enjoyed.

THE FORGOTTEN FARMSTEAD

After the Queen's College Scheme failed in 1840 Hampton Warren continued in its traditional role of providing a grazing ground for cattle, sheep and horses. It was still part of the Bathampton Estate which the Lord of the Manor, George Edward Allen, had inherited in 1785. Unlike most of his predecessors he lived in the village and took a personal interest in his Estate. He created new farms when it was fragmented by the Kennet and Avon Canal, the New Warminster Road (built by the Black Dog Turnpike Trust) and the Great Western Railway during the first half of the 19th century. At some time before 1845 he added to his personal landholdings by purchasing some Glebe Lands in Bathampton belonging to Bristol Cathedral. Most of these were fields which ran along the hillside immediately below and north-northwest of the Warren. When George Edward died in 1850 his nephew Major Ralph Shuttleworth Allen inherited the Estate. The following year he retired from the regular army and returned to the Bath area taking up a post with the North Somerset Yeomanry. He also began sorting out his new responsibilities – placing much of the management of his Estate in the hands of employees.

The grazing on the Warren required an overseer – it appears that John Ruddick of Sham Castle Cottage was appointed, holding the grazing rights and carrying out the necessary work. A track from the North Road accessed the western end of the Warren near his cottage, enabling him to count the animals in and out and collect the grazing fees. The weekly charges are detailed in advertisements he placed in the *Bath Chronicle* between 1852 and 1858, varying between one shilling and six pence for a yearling heifer and four shillings for a mare and colt.

In 1858 Major Allen retired from the Yeomanry. He then turned his attention to re-organising the land that his uncle had held, placing it into the hands of new or tenant farmers. The Warren and the old Glebe Lands below were a problem as they lay on the western side of the parish remote from Bathampton village. Apparently it was felt that this whole area was best managed as a farm with someone living on site. Sham Castle Cottage was still occupied by Ruddick who was becoming elderly and had taken on another job as Waterman – looking after the springs which fed Bath and rose on the Bathwick hillside below Sham Castle. A new farmhouse would have to be built to accommodate a Grazier to take over from him.

A site was found about half way up the steep hillside above St George's Hill (where enclosed fields then joined the open downland) on a level, sheltered strip of land, with fresh water springs nearby. In this lonely spot (OS ST 769.656) Warren Farm was built, its nearest neighbour being the Toll House which then stood at the junction of Bathampton Lane and the New Warminster Road (the A36) below. The exact date when the farmhouse was constructed is unknown; it is not on the Bathampton Census Return for 1861 but is listed in 1871 when it was occupied by Samuel King, a Grazier, his wife Lydia, and their four young children, including a two month old baby. Living with them were Lydia's widowed sister, Elizabeth Collins, and their niece, Kate Gillard. The Kings had moved to Bathampton from London some time between early summer 1867 and 26 June 1869.[1] They may well have been the first occupants but the following advertisements in the *Bath Chronicle* suggest that someone was living at Warren Farm before them:

> The first appeared weekly from 9 April to 4 June 1863, it advertised stud fees for the pedigree stallion Kingfisher, this ex-racehorse could be seen by applying to '*the owner, Mr E Smith, Hampton Warren*'.

> The second on 3 May 1866 was similar to those placed previously by Ruddick listing the grazing fees, however he was not mentioned and the entrance is now '*at the Toll Gate*'. In this case the animals would have gone up onto the Warren past the site of the new farmhouse.

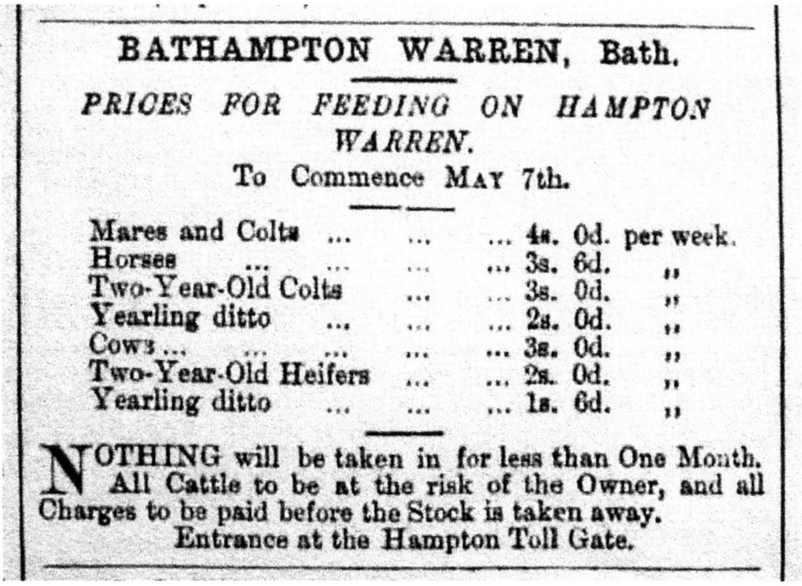

BATHAMPTON WARREN, Bath.

PRICES FOR FEEDING ON HAMPTON WARREN.

To Commence MAY 7th.

Mares and Colts	4s. 0d. per week.
Horses	3s. 6d. ,,
Two-Year-Old Colts ...	3s. 0d. ,,
Yearling ditto	2s. 0d. ,,
Cows	3s. 0d. ,,
Two-Year-Old Heifers ...	2s. 0d. ,,
Yearling ditto	1s. 6d. ,,

NOTHING will be taken in for less than One Month. All Cattle to be at the risk of the Owner, and all Charges to be paid before the Stock is taken away. Entrance at the Hampton Toll Gate.

Fig. 38 Advertisement from *Bath Chronicle*, 3 May 1866.
(By permission of the British Newspaper Archive)

The *Bath Street Directories* list the Kings at Hampton Warren from 1870 until 1873. It seems that life there did not suit them as that year they sailed for America from Liverpool, arriving in New York on 1 September. Two years later a daughter, Cecilia, was born in Connecticut but by the time they had their last child, Edward, in December 1876 they had returned to the Bathwick area. It is clear that they did not return to the farm as the 1881 census shows them living in Bedminster, where Samuel was working as a cooper – later censuses record them at Devizes and finally Lacock where Lydia died in 1921 and Samuel in 1924.

The Kings were related to James Gillard who worked the nearby 100 acre Smallcombe Farm in Bathwick. In 1868 he had married Lydia's older sister, Marion Manning, at Bathampton Church and when the Kings emigrated he took over Warren Farm from them. The *Directories* list him as Farmer at The Warren from 1874-77 but he may not have lived there as he is also listed as Farmer at Claverton Down Cottage. Two newspaper reports in the 1877 *Bath Chronicle* confirm that he was working in the area:

The first, on 30 August, reported a court case in which a local lad, Ernest Loveder, was caught snaring rabbits by James Gillard, gamekeeper, on land occupied by James Candy at Bathampton. Two local Magistrates spoke up for the boy and, as his parents were *'most respectable people'*, he was only fined two shillings and six pence.

The second, two weeks later, stated that Walter Pryor was accused of *'trespassing in search of game'* on land *'occupied by James Gillard at Hampton Warren'*. He was seen 100 yards from a footpath carrying a gun which he attempted to hide in a ditch but it was discovered later by Gillard's son Benjamin. Pryor was fined one pound (or fourteen days imprisonment) as he had been convicted of a similar offence previously.

From 1878-79 James Gillard is shown as being at Upper Norwood Farm which was also on Claverton Down. This entry is inaccurate as the *Bath Chronicle* records the sale, at Norwood Farm on 23 October 1877, of his *'stock, hay and agricultural implements'*. The farm had been put up for sale on 22 June by the owner, Henry Duncan Skrine of Claverton Manor. Major Allen who, by then, had moved into Bathampton Manor bought it to add to his Estate – it conveniently adjoined the southern boundary of the Warren. [During the twentieth century Norwood Farm was demolished – its land used for playing fields and ultimately the building of Bath University].

James Gillard, the tenant, moved back to his native village of Culmstock in Devon after the sale but had to return in December for a court case as he had not been paid for a mare sold at the auction. The horse had become violent after it was sold and the case was settled when Gillard offered to take it back.

It seems that he may have been running Warren Farm and Norwood Farm at the same time. After he moved to Culmstock the *Bath Directories* for 1880-1881 list R and J Gillard (perhaps his sons) as farmers at Hampton Warren. They must have left by the time the census was taken on 3 April 1881 as Warren Farm was not recorded – possibly it was no longer viable as the Bath Golf Club opened a nine hole course on part of the Warren that year.[2] Although the area occupied by the course still needed to be grazed by sheep and cattle to keep the grass 'mown' restrictions were imposed and farming would have been curtailed.

It is unlikely that anyone lived at the farmstead after the Gillards left as, by 27 September 1881, the Candys, farmers of Bathampton village, are recorded as tenants of *'the area of downland known as the Warren'*. The farmhouse does not appear on later Census Returns so it seems to have been used for only about 20 years (c1861-81).

The first large scale Ordnance Survey Map[3] dated 1885 shows the abandoned farmhouse, with its outbuildings, sited at the eastern corner of a small field with a large pond nearby. This was possibly a duck pond but was most likely used for watering stock as there is no water on the upper levels of Hampton Warren. Fortunately several springs rise lower down the hillside – one of these was piped to feed the pond.

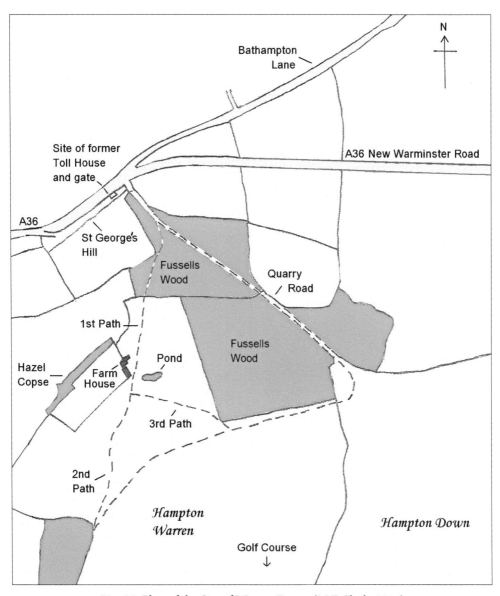

Fig. 39 Plan of the Site of Warren Farm. (M F Clark, 2014)
Based on Large Scale OS Maps of 1888 and 1904, Sheet XIV.6
(Bath Record Office)

Three paths converge near the building as seen above The first leads southwards up from St George's Hill; it is so steep here that driving a wagon up to the farmhouse would have been difficult. The second continues the climb south-west from the farm to the top of the Down. The third route gave the easiest access, as it was wide enough for a horse and cart and sloped gently south-east up the hillside, emerging onto the top beside the corner of Fussells Wood. From here it was simple to continue eastwards for a short distance, then turn downhill to join the top of the St George's Hill Track (once known as Quarry Road) to access the New Warminster Road by the Tollhouse.

The site of the farm continued to be recorded on subsequent large scale ordnance survey maps until 1936. By the mid-1950s, however, all that remained were the walls of the buildings, in a dilapidated state, complete with a few rusty nails where roses might have been tied. Intrigued by the ruins my friend and I (then two young girls in our last year at Bathampton Primary School) climbed the hill one summer day armed with trowels and forks, excitedly determined on some very amateur excavation. Inside the remains of a room we uncovered traces of a flagstone floor, a few broken red roofing tiles and, inevitably, some shards of blue and white china amongst the nettles and brambles.

In the late 1960s the area around the ruins was bulldozed as part of a clearance undertaken by the tenant farmer of the time, so that nothing can be seen now apart from the overgrown and silted up pond.

Fig. 40 The remains of Warren Farm pond.
The spring which supplied the water is in the centre.
(M F Clark, 2013)

Today the hillside is covered with trees and scrub, which make it almost impossible to imagine the grass covered lower slopes of the Down and the pleasant fields above St George's Hill full of wild flowers or the small hazel copse below the farmhouse as they were before the clearance. The three ways that led to it are now narrow footpaths, somewhat overgrown. No one would know that the Warren Farm had ever existed.

THE GOLF COURSE

A large part of the grazing land occupied by the farmstead underwent a major change of use when Bath Golf Club opened a nine hole course on the Warren. When it was first founded in 1880, the Club played at Kingsdown but this was not convenient for their Bath members and in 1881 they moved nearer to the City, leasing part of the Warren at a reasonable rent from James Candy, the tenant farmer. The Club Meeting in September of that year presents a picture of the state of the Warren – the grass was too long for play to take place. Candy gave the Club the right to '*mow 1 acre for greens, cut what bushes, bramble and thistles and do what levelling they please*'. They could also '*broadcast salt to attract cattle and during the present exceptional season cut away rough grass on the Course*'. In November the Club spent £2 14s 0d on making nine greens. Two years later a Ladies Club was formed which had its own nine hole course situated just outside the present boundary, north of today's 1st, 2nd, 3rd and 5th holes.

The first Clubhouse, a small wooden shed, was built near Sham Castle. It was sited on the Bathwick side of the parish boundary wall just above Sham Castle Cottage. In 1890 a speaking tube was installed between the shed and the cottage, enabling Club members to summon Mrs Ruddick. Not only was she in charge of the Clubhouse, providing refreshments, she also put out the flags on the greens each day and cleaned the golf clubs.

Fig. 41 Access to the Course was off the North Road, Bathwick, via what is now called Golf Course Road but was then a narrow grassy track with fields on either side, 1908. The first Clubhouse can be seen in the distance. (© Bath in Time – Dafnis Collection)

By 1893 plans to extend the Course *'on the other side of the stone wall which forms the boundary'* were being discussed at the AGM; this was the wall which divided the Warren from Hampton Down. One of James Candy's sons, either Arthur or George, was now tenanting the Down and agreed to sublet *'the whole of that ground'* to the Club for £5 per annum. The owner, Colonel Ralph Edward Allen, Major Allen's successor, consented provided the Club also paid him a nominal rent. The Links[1] were then extended to 18 holes but did not occupy the area used by the Volunteer Rifle Range on the north side of the Down as the firing posed a considerable hazard for golfers. This problem was solved when the Range was closed on safety grounds in 1894. [See pages 101-102]. Tom Dunn, the Professional at Tooting Bec, a London Club, gave advice on the lay-out of the Course but ran into difficulties with local antiquarians, who thought that the extensive prehistoric remains on the Down might be affected; fortunately for the Club agreement was reached.

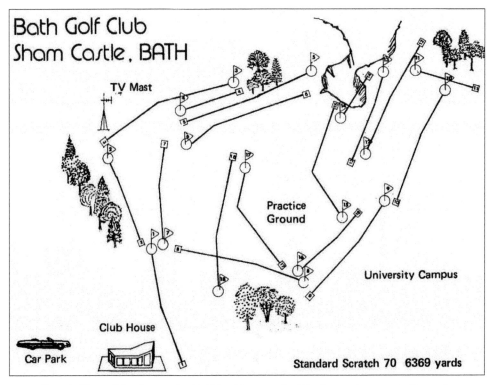

Fig. 42 Plan of the Course in 1985 looking north. The layout is very similar today except for the position of the 6th green. (Golf Club Handbook, 1985)

By the mid 1890s the Club had decided to employ a Groundsman, *'of good character to look after the Bath Links'* at a salary of one pound a week. He also gave professional advice to golfers at a cost of two shillings and six pence for a round of 18 holes. Arthur Candy was paid an extra £5 a year rent *'providing he kept all horses off except his own brood mare'* and a mole catcher had been hired. In 1899 a 21 year lease for 97 acres, comprising the Warren and the Castle Field, was negotiated with Colonel Allen at £70 per annum, together with a sub-lease from George Candy at £40 per annum. This area represented about half of the Links acreage. By 1903 the Club was negotiating a similarly long lease on the other half of the Links on Hampton Down. One of the Candy brothers then demanded an increase in rent to £20 a year. The Club agreed to this provided it could make additional greens and bunkers which would be fenced and wired in. Livestock were obviously a problem as by 1907 the Candys were being paid £12 each to curtail the number of cattle on the Course between May and October.

Ralph Edward Allen, now a Major General, died in 1910 and the Bath Golf Club became increasingly anxious about the security of its tenure. Its fears turned out to be groundless as in February, 1913, after the death of Arthur Candy, it was offered the option of leasing the whole of the area occupied by the Course directly from the Bathampton Estate at an annual rent of £130. The lease was successfully negotiated and the Club was then able to let the grazing to the new tenants of Bathampton and Norwood farms.[2]

One month later more trouble was brewing; there was a rumour that the local Suffragettes were planning a raid on the Course during the night. The police took this seriously and despatched four constables to Sham Castle as a preventative measure. The unfortunate policemen spent hours walking around the hilltop on the look-out for imaginary Suffragettes during a night of howling wind and hailstorms. The next morning an inspection of the Course showed that no damage had been done; it may have been a hoax or perhaps the police presence deterred the women from taking action.[3] Almost a year later the Suffragettes carried out their threat, during the night they cut up the turf on a number of greens, leaving luggage labels attached to the flags with slogans such as '*There can be no sport or peace until women have the vote*' and '*Militancy must go on until justice is done to women*'.[4]

Eighteen months before the First World War began champion golfer James Braid was employed to plan a number of improvements to the Course and these were carried out. The war years which followed proved a very difficult time for the Club with the deaths of a number of members on active service. Meetings and competitions were abandoned, the Club had to be run with the '*strictest economy*' and the upkeep of the Course suffered. In 1916 the Military were refused permission to train on the Down but were allowed to use the Links '*for observation purposes*' provided they left by 10.30am and did not use horses or do any damage. In the spring of the following year the Ministry of Agriculture suggested using the Course to produce food; the Club pointed out that the full extent of the land was already leased for grazing and that the poor, shallow soil was unsuitable for growing hay or crops. By September the Military had been given permission to use the Links daily for drill until 2pm; play was to continue as far as practicable without interfering with the troops. It seems likely that in fact the Course was little used – the Committee had great difficulty keeping it open for the duration of the war.

In 1921, when the Bathampton Estate was sold, Bath Golf Club was able to obtain the £4,000 needed to purchase the whole Course by raising debentures from its 356 members plus a £2,000 mortgage. Included in the sale were the Quarries to the east and a large area of rough pasture and woodland on the lower, north-western, slopes of the Down where the Warren Farm ruins still stood. Seven years later a new, much larger, Clubhouse was opened, also near Sham Castle but this time on the Bathampton side of the parish boundary wall. The

Artisan (less privileged) members were not allowed in the new building and the old shed continued in use as their Clubhouse. By 1932 Sham Castle Cottage and its garden were unoccupied – despite financial difficulties the Club did not seem to want to let it and it fell into a ruinous state. Some remains are still visible amongst the trees and undergrowth.

Fig. 43 Ladies outside the 1928 Clubhouse, c1940.
Centre: Eileen Tillett; far right Lady Katherine Cairns, Bath Ladies Captain 1938-9.
(BLHRG, Lucy Barlow Collection)

In 1937, at an Extraordinary General Meeting, the Club resolved that as it *'possessed 240 acres of ground with good turf, varying contours, and almost unique natural hazards'* it would employ Harry S Colt, the legendary golf architect, to make various improvements. He re-planned the Course abolishing blind spots on several holes, increasing the length by 500 yards, making six new greens, and constructing sand bunkers to replace ancient turf banks and hollows. As a result the Course gained a very good reputation and an increase in the number of members and visitors.

The outbreak of World War II in 1939 inevitably changed this state of affairs and the Course became partially neglected. In 1940 the Committee agreed to a request, from the War Agriculture Sub-Committee for Bathampton, to allow George Candy to graze sheep on the Course. The farmer stated that getting wire to fence sheep was impossible and suggested young cattle instead. He relented when a new agreement was struck – he was to provide fencing for sheep on the Course and the Club would not charge him rent while the war lasted. A local resident who often walked over the Down with her dog in those days said that, because of the peace and beauty of her surroundings, she found it almost impossible to believe a war was taking place.

Soon after the war the Course was restored to its former excellent condition, and by the late 1940s was described as having '*perfect springy turf on shallow soil covering natural rock, ensuring rapid drying even after heavy rain*'. Apart from its '*grand sporting facilities*' there were glorious views from certain tees, '*embracing the City, the Downs that encircle it, Bathford, Warleigh Manor and Woods*', its '*serene air, sense of detachment, and beautiful surroundings*' proved attractive to many golfers. Photographs of the time show an extremely bare downland course, almost devoid of trees and shrubs and with open views to the north, east and west.

Fig. 44 View from the 5th green looking north, c1950. Bathampton Church and Batheaston in the centre distance. (BLHRG, Lucy Barlow Collection)

By April 1951 the number of walkers wandering '*aimlessly over the fairways and greens oblivious of the risks they are taking*' had increased and the Club inserted a notice in the *Bath Chronicle* warning the public of the danger, asking them to keep to the footpaths and stating that although they did not wish to curtail their enjoyment the Golf Course was in fact private property. Although the footpaths are now clearly marked the same problem exists today.

One local golfer who must be mentioned is the late Miss Lucy Barlow of Bathampton Lane; like her father before her she played on the Course for many years. In 1956 she became Ladies Captain, a position which she held six times in all. Her interest in the history of

Bathampton led to her family making a gift from her estate which has funded several history projects in the village. Her collection of photographs illustrates the Bath Golf Club members and the Course on which they played, particularly during the 1930s, 40s and 50s.

Fig. 45 Lady Katherine Cairns (4th from left) and Lucy Barlow (5th from left) with friends on the 1st fairway – Sham Castle in the distance – possibly 1930s or early 1940s. (BLHRG, Lucy Barlow Collection)

Today the par 71 Course is 6,500 yards long and still occupies the same area perched high on top of Bathampton Down but there have been some changes. In 1965 a small area of rough pasture, just outside the north-west boundary, was sold for the erection of a television mast – a further mast has been added since. In 1971 a new Clubhouse was built next to the old one. The 1928 Clubhouse still exists but is now used for changing rooms and staff accommodation – the Artisan's shed is long gone as is the Ladies Course which closed in 1921 when they were permitted to play on the Men's Course. In 1996 part of the Sham Castle Field was leased for use as a warm up area and later became a driving range. The appearance of what was once called 'the Links' is greatly changed as many trees have been planted, including some groups of firs reminiscent of those put in by Ralph Allen. It no longer has the bare appearance of former years and many of the panoramic views have been obscured by the growth of trees there and on the slopes below. Officially called the Bath Golf Club Course it is often affectionately known by local players as 'Sham' owing to the proximity of Ralph Allen's folly, a depiction of which forms the Club logo, as seen here.

PART TWO

The Eastern Side of the Wall –

HAMPTON DOWN

Fig. 46 View of the northern slopes of Hampton Down, c1932.
(© Bath in Time – Dafnis Collection)

The remains of the Hampton Down Quarries can be seen on the skyline. The woodland below the quarries has not yet encroached on the open downland to their right. Development of the lower slopes of the hillside has begun with houses in Down Lane and ribbon development on both sides of the Warminster Road. New bungalows line the lower side of Devonshire Road but those on the upper side are not yet built. Harbutt's Plasticene Factory can be seen centre left with The Normans behind it.

THE QUARRIES

Section I
Winning the Stone

For centuries Bath Stone was quarried on Bathampton Down. It has been called '*a material which in truth is fit for the walls of a Palace for the greatest Prince in Europe*'.[1] Lying below the tops of the hills which curve around Bath it is a sedimentary rock formed from small grains compacted to make beds of oolitic limestone. The boundaries, or bedding plains, between these together with cracks formed as the layers of sediment dried out, indicate where it is easy to remove blocks of the best quality stone. Known as freestone, as it can be sawn in any direction, this is honey-coloured underground and can be cut with a hand saw – as it is so soft it must be exposed to the air in stacking yards for some time to harden before use.

Fig. 47 *Free Stone Quarries near Bath.*
Drawn and engraved by J Hassell, 1798. Thought to be on Hampton Down.
(Victoria Art Gallery, Bath & North East Somerset Council)

Most of the quarries are situated to the south and east of the City, including those on Bathampton Down which appear to have been excavated by the same methods used elsewhere in the region. A quarry was started by a roughly arc-shaped area, often on the edge of the hillside, being cleared of topsoil, subsoil and poor quality stone which could be used for rough walling. The beds of valuable freestone were then exposed below. The work was done by hand and as it progressed, ate into the hill – the spoil was tipped behind. The working faces advanced very laboriously by a sequence of picking, sawing and breaking out blocks, using the natural faults in the stone.

As work continued the broad level floor created, which could be used for the stacking yard, often developed into an 'amphitheatre'. The surrounding cliffs could be 50 or 60 feet high and usually had horizontal shafts running into the hillside following beds of freestone. These sometimes ran for a considerable distance underground, branching out in different directions, with columns of stone remaining to support the roof.

The old stone workers referred to all places where stone was dug as quarries whether they were above or below ground. Their life was extremely hard; for example a sawyer, employed to cut the large blocks of stone, worked a ten hour day and is estimated to have made, in that day, 30,000 forward and backward strokes. Underground the men worked by candlelight and accidents were common. They became covered in powdered stone and were easily recognised on their way to and from work as they tied their trousers with a leather strap below the knee to keep the upper part loose, which made it easier to kneel.

Quarry owners employed foremen (gangers) to get the stone, paying them fortnightly for work done. The men supplied their own tools and candles. The owners provided other equipment including cranes, known to have been used in opencast quarrying in the mid 1700s,[2] but not introduced underground until the 1820s. After the stone had hardened it could be transported to stone masons' yards elsewhere or cut on site. At the bigger quarries sawyers trimmed the large blocks; if required they could also cut them into smaller sizes. They were then dressed by the free (banker) masons at the quarry, working in open sided sheds with stone or thatched roofs. These Ashlar blocks were then ready for transportation to the rough masons (bricklayers) who used them for building purposes, such as the houses of Georgian Bath.

Development of the Bathampton Quarries

Those enjoying the peace and fresh air on the Down today will find it hard to imagine the noisy, dirty, industrial scene which was the Hampton Down Quarries at the height of their activity in the early 19th century. The main area of quarrying, now known locally as Hampton Rocks, on the north-eastern heights of the Down was extensive; the largest quarry was the one which became known as the Seven Sisters as it had seven tunnel entrances at the far western end (OS ST 777.654).

The following illustration of this very large working shows the bridleway running north to south from Bathampton to Claverton Down. Some of the extensive remains of the pre-historic field system which exists on Hampton Down can also be seen. The embankment of the Iron Age enclosure is shown running westwards from the far end of the quarry to the top of the photograph.

Fig. 48 Aerial view of the Seven Sisters Quarry looking west. North Quarry, with its track joining the bridleway, can be seen to its right. (West Air Photography, 1976)

Quarries had been opened nearby in much earlier times. The Romans, who were experienced in quarrying and mining, were probably the first to exploit the valuable resource of the stone lying under the local hilltops on a large scale. They used it to develop their important regional and leisure centre of Aquae Sulis (i.e. Bath) with temples and baths and also to build villas in the surrounding countryside. There is no evidence that they quarried stone on Bathampton Down but it is believed that there are remains of Roman workings just over the parish boundary in Bathwick Woods.[3]

It is thought that the earliest quarries were made into the side of the hilltop[4] at its northeastern end. The first documentary evidence of such quarrying on the Down dates to 1479 when the Churchwardens of St Michael's, Bath, paid ten shillings and eight pence for eight loads of stone from '*Hamptonys quarra*' to be used for two rooms at a tenement in Broad Street.[5] Almost a hundred years later on 10 April 1564 at the Court of William Button, Lord of the Manor of Bathampton, four of his tenants, '*the homage*', were sworn in and discussed the case of John Burde of Bath who '*unjustly and without a licence from the Lord, has carried away a cartload of stone, namely freestone, within the jurisdiction of this court, in the place called Hampton Quarre*'.[6] Unfortunately the penalty is not recorded.

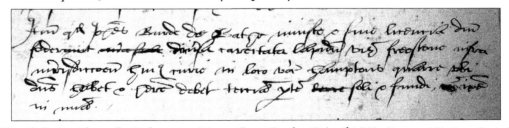

Fig. 49 Extract from the Bathampton Manor Court Books 10 April 1564. (Somerset Heritage Centre)

In 1726, almost two centuries later, the entrepreneur Ralph Allen acquired the quarries on Combe Down. These provided good quality stone for the rapid development of housing in Bath. On 24 March 1736 he married Elizabeth Holder, the niece[6a] of Charles Holder, the Lord of Bathampton Manor. Allen, an astute businessman, already had an interest in the Manor and may have begun developing the old Bathampton workings in about 1730. It is likely that he would have wished to utilize all the assets of the Manor, which he finally acquired in 1742-43, including the stone quarries – however the only evidence for this is an unreliable account by local historian R E M Peach in 1895.[7] This describes how nearly all the stone from the Quarries *'was hewn in the open, dressed with much care and laid by for seasoning'*. He then relates how Allen built two tramways; one in 1731 to convey stone from Combe Down to his riverside Wharf at Widcombe, the other at about the same time *'in connection with Hampton Down'*. There *'a series of short trams were laid on to a centre where was constructed a large drum worked by some kind of machinery'*. He also states that a tramway was built from the drum extending along the Down, this descended the slope to the edge of a steep gorge where the stone was unloaded and conveyed to Allen's stoneyard and basin.

Peach's record is unfounded, he may have confused a simple arrangement of short lengths of tramway within Allen's quarry with the more sophisticated mechanism of a tramway built in 1808, which will be described later. If there was an early tramway, no real evidence of it remains. There is a possibility that one of the man-made trackways on the north slopes of the Down might be part of its course. This leads to the track to St George's Hill[8] which is called Quarry Road on a plan for the proposed Kennet and Avon Canal dated 1797.[9]

Fig. 50 Extract from the 1797 Plan showing Quarry Road. (Somerset Heritage Centre)

If Allen did open quarries at Bathampton in the 1730s such an enterprise may have been short lived as he was developing his very successful Combe Down Workings at about the same time. His Estate Map of c1740-64 and Thorpe's Map of 1742 both show the Combe Down workings but there are no quarries indicated on Bathampton Down. In addition, Allen, who was known as 'The Benevolent Man', provided terraces of cottages for his workers at Combe Down and Widcombe, but did not do so at Bathampton where the only similar developments are Chapel Row and Canal Terrace, which were built at a later date.

During the late eighteenth and early nineteenth centuries several famous artists were inspired by the rugged, romantic scenery of the Quarries and the extensive, beautiful views from their hilltop site. Foremost amongst these was Thomas Gainsborough, who lived in Bath from 1759 to 1774; he made his living painting portraits of the rich and famous who came to the City in winter for 'the season'. In summer he was free to indulge his love of landscape painting, riding to the hills around Bath each afternoon to make preparatory sketches for his compositions. He was often seen at Hampton Rocks where he ate his 'rustic meal' on a flat rock which became known locally as Gainsborough's Pallet or Table.[10] Perhaps this was the flat topped stack now called the Devil's Table, Pulpit or Dancing Stool. His *Rocky Wooded Landscape with Rustic Lovers, Herdsmen and Cows*, which was probably inspired by the rocky outcrops of Hampton Down and Kingsdown, is one of two paintings he thought were his best. It is held by the National Museum of Wales.

Fig. 51 The Devil's Table, c1920. (© Bath in Time - Dafnis Collection)

Gainsborough probably inspired another well known artist, Thomas Barker (1769-1847) who lived in Bath, to paint the rugged heights and crags of the Quarries. His oil painting *Hampton Rocks Morning* showing a large outcrop of rock with a shepherd and his flock in the foreground is held by the Victoria Art Gallery in Bath. The stunning scenery also inspired the famous American artist Benjamin West (1738-1820) who stayed in the City during 1807. On his return to London he said '*Take Bath and twenty miles round it and there is not in the world anything superior to it. Rocks of the finest forms for a painter that I have ever seen with large square forms, quarries worked out, now most picturesque and romantic'.*[11]

For centuries stone needed for buildings in Bathampton village was probably quarried on Hampton Down as the difficulties of transport over bad roads necessitated it being sourced from the nearest convenient place. There is evidence of its use in the Bathampton Highway Accounts, for example, on 12 February 1785,[12] a man named Cornish was paid £3 for *'diging 120 loads of stone'*. On 28 May Isack Bevin was paid 18 shillings for *'breaking 36 loads of stones'* and John Holborough 8s 6d for *'breaking 13 loads'*.

These poor quality stones were used for road-mending as at that time each parish was responsible for the upkeep of roads within its boundaries. Vestry committees appointed two villagers as surveyors of the highways each year; unpaid and unpopular posts. All able-bodied parishioners had to give a certain number of days labour annually on the roads and often had to pick stones from the fields for this purpose. In Bathampton, where sub-standard stone was readily available from the Quarries, this may not have been the case. It is also known that Ralph Allen used discarded weathered rocks from his quarries to construct 10 miles of rides on his Estate during the mid 18th century.

It is doubtful whether Cornish had time to admire his surroundings while he was busy digging all those loads of stone but perhaps he glanced around him as he drove his cart back down the steep track to the village. We may imagine what he saw from the description given by Edmund Rack in his *Survey of Somerset*, written at the time.[13] *'The eastern point of the hill called Hampton Cliffs is nearly 700 feet above the river and from its steepness almost inaccessible. Its brow is strongly contrasted by rugged projecting rocks and quarries, and plantations of firs, beneath which fine hanging coppice woods extend almost to the bottom. From this elevated spot the prospects are highly romantic and beautifully diversified with everything essential to the perfection of scenery'.*

By the late 18th century the Quarries were in decline. In 1785 George Edward Allen became Lord of the Manor, two years later the valuation of his property stated that *'The privilege of getting stone or opening quarries on the Common Down'* has frequently brought in an income of £15 or £16 a year but the present rent is only £5.[14]

The Quarries expand and prosper

Twenty years later the situation was very different; the Quarries were re-opened and a period of major expansion began. On 22 April 1808, George Edward Allen leased the rights to *'all the beds, veins and quarries of stone mine, metals and minerals… under or upon Bathampton Down'*, probably to The Bathampton Free-Stone Quarry Company. This lease does not survive but is mentioned in another dated 14 November 1817,[15] granted by Allen to Richard Bowsher, an eminent Bath Solicitor who was involved in a number of similar operations and seems to have been associated with the Quarry Company. Bowsher was granted the new lease, which included an extra 18 acres of land between the Quarry and the Canal, for

23 years. He had the option of termination at nine or 16 years and agreed to pay rent of £241 5s 0d for the first 16 years and £441 5s 0d for the last seven years. He was allowed to operate in a designated area which was '*situate on the left hand side of the parish road leading from the village of Bathampton to the gate at the enclosure of Bathampton Down, extending… in a line round the summit of the Down to the prospect stile and between such points… and the Manor of Claverton*' but could also follow any veins of stone or minerals under George Edward Allen's adjoining land. Permission was given for him to remove earth or stone as necessary to open and work the Quarries, make tunnels, shafts and pits, use engines and machines, set up buildings and forges and prepare stone for sale. Bowsher had free access for his workmen, horses and carts and could make roads, paths, and railroads anywhere in the designated area, but he was not allowed to '*use the public parish road in conveying stone from his quarry*'.

Fig. 52 Richard Bowsher's signature on the lease of 1817. (Bath Record Office)

The reason for the major expansion in 1808 was the construction of the Kennet and Avon Canal, which had already opened locally and was finally completed for through traffic in 1810. It ran along the Limpley Stoke Valley only a mile below the Hampton Down Quarries. The Canal Company had been using stone for building the Canal from Conkwell, Winsley, Westwood and Bradford on Avon, however the quality was found to be poor and by 1802 better stone was being sourced for the very expensive job of replacing it. In that year a site on Claverton Down was surveyed for a new quarry with a tramway leading from it to the Canal but this development did not materialise.[16]

The Hampton Down Quarry, which re-opened six years later, was ideally situated to supply the Company with the quality of stone it required for the replacement work, however there is no documentary evidence that it did so. The Bathampton Free-Stone Quarry Company may simply have decided to take advantage of the commercial opportunities which the Kennet and Avon Canal offered. They knew that when the waterway was completed it would provide their newly opened Quarry with an easy and convenient method of transporting the stone blocks for sale, west to Bristol and east to London.

> ### BATH FREE-STONE QUARRIES.
>
> BARGE Owners are requested to make Tenders of the terms on which they will convey Stone per ton from ABINGDON or READING to LONDON, and also to OXFORD and other places on the THAMES.
>
> The BATHAMPTON FREE-STONE QUARRY COMPANY inform the public, that these Quarries are re-opened so as to afford an extensive supply of the best stone; they will communicate, by an inclined plane, about two miles from Bath, with the Kennett and Avon Canal, and from thence, by the Wilts and Berks Canal, with the THAMES, at ABINGDON, where, and in LONDON, the Stone may be delivered by contract.—The Bathampton Free-Stone for all purposes of solid, useful, and ornamental building, cisterns, pipes, &c. for durability and the facility and cheapness of cleaning and working it, in all the branches of masonry, has preference over Portland, Painswick, and every other Stone hitherto discovered in Europe.
>
> It can be delivered in London considerably under the price of Portland Stone, and may be worked at a very considerable less expence.
>
> The Tenders of Barge Owners, and other applications, by letter, addressed to the Bathampton Free-Stone Quarry Company, Bath, will have due attention.

Fig. 53 Advertisement from *Jackson's Oxford Journal*, 22 July 1809.
(By permission of the British Newspaper Archive)

Fig. 54 The Devil's Quarry, a typical view of underground workings.
(Courtesy of David Grosvenor, 2010)

THE QUARRIES

Section II
Transportation – The Tramway

To maximise profits it was necessary to provide a quick and cheap method of transporting stone from the Quarry to the Canal below, it was therefore decided to build a self-acting inclined plane, half a mile long, straight down the steep hillside. This was a precursor of the modern railway, called a tramroad or tramway, known locally as a dramway. It was double tracked and needed no power source as the weight of the laden wagons descending on one track pulled up the empty ones ascending on the other. At the bottom of the tramway a Wharf was to be constructed at the Canal-side so that the stone could be off-loaded directly onto waiting barges.

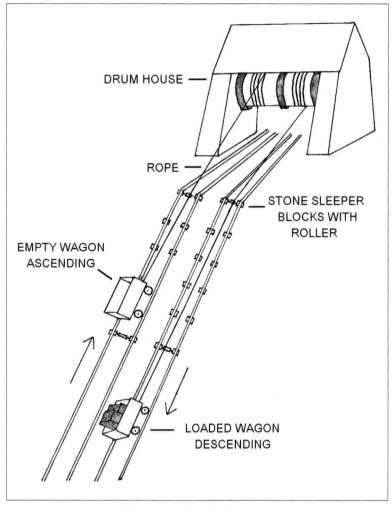

DRUM HOUSE

ROPE

STONE SLEEPER
BLOCKS WITH
ROLLER

EMPTY WAGON
ASCENDING

LOADED WAGON
DESCENDING

Fig. 55 A self-acting inclined plane. (M F Clark, 2015)

Despite the financial burden of building the tramway (similar lines at that time cost upwards of £2,000 per mile) the Quarry should have soon been in profit owing to the savings made by avoiding the costly, slow and difficult option of road haulage.

> Various types of tramways had been operating in and around quarries for many years. The earliest, known as wagon-ways, had wooden rails and sleepers. These would have been used for the track mentioned previously, constructed by Ralph Allen in the mid 1700s. During the 1790s wooden tracks were phased out as more durable stone blocks and cast-iron rails came into use. Railways were developing rapidly, both nationally and locally, with tramways being built to the Canal from quarries at Conkwell and Murhill as well as from Hampton Down. At about this time Benjamin Outram of Derbyshire published his paper *Minutes to be observed in the construction of railways*; some of his instructions appear to have been applied when building the Bathampton tramway.
>
> By the 1820s the construction of inclined planes had been developed to a fine art and Britain was at the forefront of railway technology. In 1826-27 two young German engineers, Carl von Oeynhausen and Heinrich von Dechen, visited England and Wales and made meticulous notes on a number of early rail tracks so that they could help to establish similar enterprises in their own country. They included a detailed description of the Hampton Down tramway on which some of this account is based.[17]

Having decided to build the tramway, plans were drawn up and an advertisement for a contractor appeared in the *Bath Chronicle* of 23 June 1808. The massive task of constructing the line must have started soon afterwards with some areas having to be levelled or built up to provide the necessary straight, smooth incline which, when completed, was 2,658 feet long and had a perpendicular height of 480 to 500 feet (an average gradient of one in five).

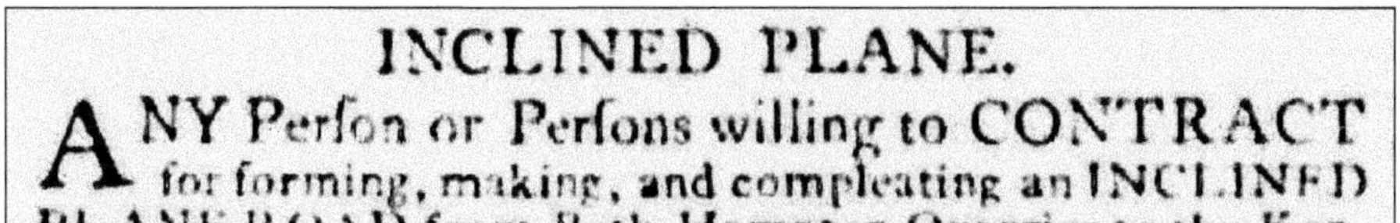

INCLINED PLANE.

ANY Perſon or Perſons willing to CONTRACT for forming, making, and compleating an INCLINED PLANE ROAD from Bath-Hampton Quarries to the Kennet and Avon Canal, a diſtance of about 800 yards, are deſired to ſend their propoſals (ſealed up) to Mr. Bennett, engineer, St. James's parade, Bath.—Plans, ſections, and ſpecifications, may be ſeen at Mr. Bennett's office.

Fig. 56 Advertisement from the *Bath Chronicle*, 23 June 1808.
(By permission of the British Newspaper Archive)

The diagram below illustrates the completed inclined plane and shows its features which are described in detail in the following text.

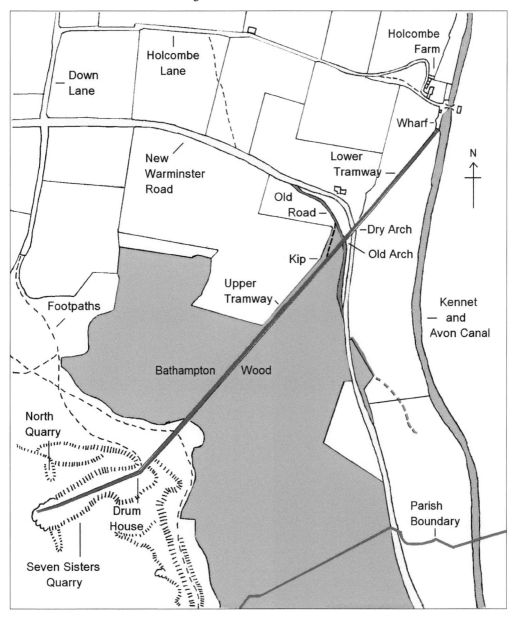

Fig. 57 Plan of the Inclined Plane constructed 1808-1809.
Based on large scale OS Maps of 1888 and 1904, Sheet XIV 6. (Bath Record Office)

Key:	Inclined Plane	Purple
	Kennet and Avon Canal	Blue
	Old Parish Road	Orange
	Parish Boundary	Red
	Roads	Yellow

In March 1809 a problem arose as the Canal Western Sub-committee objected to the site of the proposed Wharf and gave notice to the Bathampton Stone Company to *'desist from making the wharf in the said situation'*.[18] The issue must have been resolved as the Wharf survives today, at the bottom of the tramway, beside the Canal (OS ST 782.659).

Fig. 58 Bathampton Wharf, where stone was loaded onto barges;
the tramway was at the far end (M F Clark, 2011)

The *Bath Guide*[19] of that year tells us that *'The introduction of Canals… frequently gives rise to spirited exertion and enterprise… this may be seen in the extensive quarries at Hampton Down, now working by Messrs Bowsher and Co, whence immense quantities of stone are intended to be conveyed by means of an inclined plane to the Canal in the vale below'*. The *Guide* for the following year, 1810, carries the same report but states that the stone is being conveyed; giving us an estimated date of late 1809 for the opening of the tramway, which probably resembled the Penydarren Plateway (built nine years previously in South Wales in accordance with Outram's instructions).

Once the incline had been formed and drained, the bed of the track firmed and covered with beaten down gravel or small stones, the stone blocks, or sleepers, could be laid. These were not long enough to tie the lines of rail to gauge so each line had its own sleepers giving four rows of blocks (for the double track) running down the hillside. Their centres were 30 inches apart, this being the length of each rail. Over 4,000 stones were needed, each one at least 8 inches thick and weighing 150 pounds or more. They were probably supplied from the Quarry above, where they were cut and prepared by hand – the cost of similar blocks made elsewhere in 1811 for the Kilmarnock and Troon Railway, Scotland, was sixpence each.

Their shape was immaterial as long as they had a flat bottom to rest on; they had to be firmly fixed with no earth between them and the gravel bed. Part of the upper surface had to be level enough for a 5 inch groove to be cut to form a firm bed for the ends of the rails. A hole 1½ inches in diameter and 6 inches deep was drilled in the centre of each block to take an octagonal oak plug which was shorter than the hole to allow for expansion when wet. An iron spike with a square pyramidal head was driven into this plug to fix the countersunk, notched rail ends to the block.

Fig. 59 Stone sleeper block showing rail fixings – due to much erosion it now stands proud of its original bedding. (G M Huggins, 2012)

The Hampton Down line was a tramway or plateway – one on which the 'L' section, cast iron plate rails had a flange on the inner edge to keep the plain wheels of the wagons on the track. Plateways usually had rails 3 feet long but for some reason those used at Bathampton were shorter. Oeynhausen and Dechen describe them as being 2½ feet long, 3½ inches wide and ⅝ of an inch thick, with a flange 2½ inches high which was laid inwards. They were strengthened in the middle by increasing the thickness of the base by 1 inch, tapering to nothing at the ends. The ends of each rail were notched so that when they were placed against the following rail a hole was formed, through which they could be nailed to the plug in the stone sleeper. There was also a small semi-circular protrusion at one side of the end of each rail which slotted into a correspondingly shaped addition to the groove in the stone; this helped to hold the rail in place. '*The gauge of each track is 3 feet 4 inches and they lie the same distance from one another*'.

The number of rails needed was well over 4,000 (the same as the blocks), it is not known where they were manufactured. They may have come from the Coalbrookdale Ironworks in Shropshire which had been casting rails since 1767, although they did not come into general use until the 1790s. The expense must have been considerable – rails made for the Kilmarnock and Troon line, which were 3 feet long, cost just under six shillings each.

A broken piece of rail from the Bathampton Tramway. (BLHRS Collection)

Fig. 60 (Above) Cross section showing the 'L' shaped flange, notch and curved addition.

Fig. 61 (Below) The same rail viewed from above.

Cast iron is notoriously brittle and the German engineers commented that '*The rails are too weak for the load which is lowered onto them – 80 cwt including the wagon. This is proved by the large heaps of broken rails that lie beside the line; but the newly delivered ones are cast no stronger*'. However, from the remains of the few rails that have been found, it appears that three more substantial types did come into use later; each had a significant increase in size to try to cure the breakage problem.[20]

The old tramway (now a public footpath) can still be found running down the hillside; unfortunately it is becoming badly eroded. Over most of its length the two central rows of sleeper blocks are still visible – giving the misleading impression that this was only a single line. Encroaching undergrowth at each side of the track has hidden almost all of the blocks which formed the two outer rows. Some can still be found in places, proving that there was a double tramway as stated by Oeynhausen and Dechen. In places extra blocks, without fixing holes but with a deep groove to give more support to the centre of the rail, were inserted.

Fig. 62 Sleeper with an extra supporting block. (R F Pickford, 1975)

Long or steep inclines such as that at Hampton Down had to be worked in two parts, the weight of the ropes or chain which hauled the wagons and the gradient of the slope being the factors governing the length of each section. Crossing switches (presumably a system of points) were provided on both lines at the Quarry, for each of the brake arrangements, and below at the Canal.

The Upper Section

Oeynhausen and Dechen report that the upper section of the track is '*1,658 feet long and not of uniform slope; it is very little at the top, up to 10 degrees in the middle and at the bottom is both inclined and curved*'.

On checking this measurement against the large scale Ordinance Survey Map of 1888 it appears that the tramway would have extended part way into the Seven Sisters Quarry by 1826, although no remains of stone sleepers are visible in this area today. There is only a very slight slope from this point to the lip of the gorge which confirms the description of it being '*very little at the top*'. It has been suggested that this part of the tramway was on the route of Ralph Allen's original line.

Fig. 63 A Drumhouse near Dinorwig, Gwynned. (© Eric Jones, 2006)

Fig. 64 An Inclined Plane in the Retisoara Valley, Hungary, 1905. (Wikipedia)

At the head of the tramway would have stood the drumhouse – a roofed shed with substantial side walls but open at the front and back. Suspended on a horizontal axle just below the roof was the 11 feet wide, 5 feet in diameter rope drum, leaving room for the wagons to pass through on the rails below. The centre of the wooden drum was encircled by a narrow band which increased its diameter to 6 feet at that point. This divided the drum and around each half was conversely wound a 1¼ inch diameter untarred rope. These ran over wooden friction rollers 34 inches long and 6 inches in diameter, set at intervals down the track between the stone sleepers, to which they were fixed with iron pivots. A wagon laden with stone was attached to the rope on one side of the drum – as it started to roll down the sloping track it caused the drum to rotate and pull up the empty wagon attached to the rope on its other side.

On one side of the drum was a horizontal brake wheel which the brakesman used to control the speed of the heavy wagon once it passed over the lip of the gorge and descended the steepest part of the track, and to stop it when it reached the bottom end of the upper section. There was probably a signalman, whose job it was to communicate with the workers who attached and detached the wagons there. He would have been stationed at the top of the gorge, perhaps on a tower, so that he could see down the track and let the brakesman know when to apply the brake. Owing to the surrounding trees it is not possible to check whether this was feasible; if not, another system such as ringing a bell may have been used.

From the lip of the gorge the middle of this section sloped very steeply. The bottom part was less steep; Oeynhausen and Dechen's description of it as being *both inclined and curved* is somewhat puzzling as the whole tramway clearly runs in a straight line. However the answer probably lies in the construction of a Kip which provided an area where the Upper Section of tramway met the Lower.

Fig. 65 The lower part of the upper section – looking north-east down towards the Kip in the distance.
(M F Clark, 2012)

The Kip

This was a hump in the trackway which made a flat area where wagons could be switched from one haulage system to the next; it can still be seen at the point where the footpath from the Warminster Road (A36) joins the tramway. Measurements, checked against the 1888 OS Map, confirm that the switchover point was here. Crossing switches were provided and each track probably curved out around the machinery necessary at this point, coming together again below it. P J Ransom described how the changeover worked *'Ascending wagons have to be hauled over the kip on to a slight reverse gradient so that they run forward into the 'dish' and the cable slackens and can be detached, the cable from the upper section of track can then be attached for the continued ascent. Descending wagons have to stand on a slight down gradient, so that they roll as soon as the brakes are released'.*[21]

In 1819 Pierce Egan wrote a vivid description of this after walking back to Bath from Bradford on Avon: *'Proceeding some distance down the river on the left side of which an iron rail-way, from an immense steep height, is to be seen. It is curious to observe the iron carriages sent up and down, without horses; and by the aid of machinery the vehicles change their positions midway, the full one running down to the barge in the Canal, and the empty one making its way to the top again to receive its load'.*[22] The Bathampton Tithe Map of 1844 shows a small square building on the Kip, adjacent to the track on its eastern side. This may have been the brakeman's hut from which he operated the machinery which worked the lower section of track.

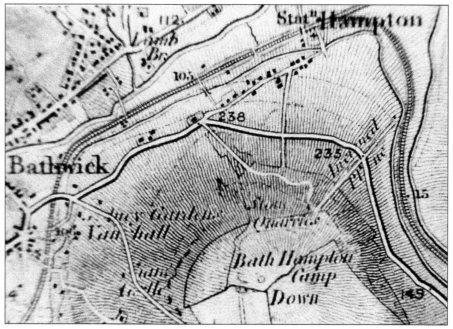

Fig. 66 The Inclined Plane and Quarry Road.
Detail from the first OS Map of 1817, rev. ed. c1860. (Bath Record Office)

The Lower Section

This part of the track ran straight down from the Kip to the Canal Wharf and was 1,000 feet long, with a uniform inclination of about five per cent. On the Kip was situated the machinery which hauled the wagons up and down; it worked on the same gravity principle as that at the top of the Upper Section but was constructed quite differently. Instead of a rope it used an iron chain with links 4½ inches long and 2¼ inches wide. This passed around a cast iron rope sheave (a grooved wheel) lying at the level of the rails on an upright shaft with a tilt of 6 inches. This sheave had a diameter of 6 feet 8 inches so that the chain ran down the centre of each pair of tramlines. Under it lay the 9 foot diameter, 8 inch high brake wheel, with jointed wooden brake-checks around three quarters of its circumference; these were drawn tight when the brake was applied. To prevent it dragging on the ground the chain ran over 9 inch diameter cast-iron friction sheaves set on separate stone sleepers (24 feet apart) in the middle of each track.

Fig. 67 The Tramway leading down to the
Canal Wharf. Holcombe Farm seen
on the left. (R F Pickford, 1975)

Fig. 68 Looking up the Tramway from
the south end of the Wharf.
(R F Pickford, 1975)

Just below the Kip a stone arch had to be built to carry the tramway over the rough parish road which was the only route from Bathampton to Claverton at that time. This arch can still be found among the trees a few yards south-west of the present Warminster Road (A36).

Fig. 69 The Old Arch over the original parish road, looking west. (G M Huggins, 2012)

It has been repaired with brick in places but is now in a somewhat ruinous state. Underneath the arch the rough protruding stonework makes it difficult to take measurements but, approximately, the span is 14 feet and the height underneath the centre of the bridge 9 feet. The width is about 18 feet, the usual breadth of bed for a double tramway, allowing a 3 foot walkway on either side of the tracks as they ran over the bridge.

The old road to Claverton fell out of use after the Black Dog Turnpike Trust opened a new road from Warminster to Bath in 1836. During the building a deep cutting was made just north of the original arch, forming a sharp bend underneath the area where the tramway ran, necessitating the construction of a further arch to carry it over the new road. This was larger than the earlier one, very well built of Bath Stone, with a sloping top to accommodate the descent of the tramway.

The Black Dog Trust placed an advertisement in the *Bath Chronicle* of 17 and 24 March 1836 inviting Contractors, Stone Masons and Others to tender for '*building a Dry Arch for an intended Railroad to lead from the Stone Quarries of George Edward Allen, across the new Turnpike Road, near Bathampton*'.

Fig. 70 The later 'Dry Arch' over the A36, looking northwards, c1950s.
(W Mannings – Harbutt Collection)

The term 'Dry Arch' can be explained in two ways; the arch did not cross over water or the masonry forming the semi-circle of the archway was of a dry-stone construction i.e. no mortar was used. Someone who watched its eventual demolition stated that the latter was the case.

For over a hundred years the later Dry Arch was a much loved local landmark and in 1958 many people were sorry when it had to be demolished so that the road could be widened and the bend made safer. It was so strongly built that it proved very difficult to knock down. The work took place on Sunday 28 January, when the walls and other pieces were removed and the following Sunday, 4 February, when the arch itself was demolished – not without a struggle – for it took several attacks with a ball on the crane before it finally gave way.

Fig. 71 Demolition of the Dry Arch, 1958. (BLHRG – W Morris Collection)

The Canal Wharf

At the bottom end of the Lower Section of tramway was the Canal Wharf. Here the waterway was made wider to allow barges to lie next to the stone built quayside. The tramlines ran down to join the Wharf at its southern end – it is not known whether they extended northwards along the quay or stopped short when they reached it. Crossing switches were provided somewhere at this end of the line, presumably on a level area where the wagons could be unhitched. The stone may have been unloaded by crane on the Wharf; alternatively the front section of each wagon may have been hinged, so that it could be lifted and the stone blocks slid into the barge by tipping the wagon on end. (Such wagons carried limestone on the Peak Forest Tramway in Derbyshire). The wagons would then be 'switched' and made ready to be hauled back to the Quarry.

The Wagons

Oeynhausen and Dechen describe those used at Hampton Down as having a wooden platform with an iron railing 2½ feet high. The platform had 4 frame beams 7½ feet long, 7 inches high and 5 inches thick, bound together by four 8 inch square cross beams and iron cramps. The cast iron axles were 40 inches apart at their centres. This ensured that as the back wheel came onto the end of each 30 inch rail, the front wheel would already be on the next rail, thus spreading the weight of the loaded wagon. The wheels had 6 spokes, were 16½ inches high and had rims 1 inch thick – these narrow wheels contributed to the number of broken rails. Each wagon weighed 10 hundredweight and carried up to 70 hundredweight of stone. There may have been only one wagon at a time on each track or 'trains' of two or more wagons hitched together; from Egan's description it seems that the former is more likely.

Fig. 72 A Peak Forest Wagon. It has wooden frames, an iron body and an open end closed by a hinged grille. The wheels, rails and sleeper blocks are very similar to those at Bathampton. (© National Railway Museum, York)

Egan's view of the tramway in 1819 would have been quite different to that of today. The illustration below shows how trees now obscure the long clearing made through the woodland for the Upper Tramway (A to B). The Lower Tramway (B to C) which once ran down through open fields to the Canal, is also hidden by trees and bushes.

Fig. 73 View from Bathford Hill looking west.
A – Quarry; B – Dry Arch; C – Wharf . (M F Clark, 2016)

THE QUARRIES

Section III
Decline and Closure

Owing to the success of the tramway the Quarries were still in full production in 1817 when the *New Bath Guide* reported that '*The Bath stone is obtained from all the hills round the city; but that from Combe Down, Claverton, and Hampton Downs, is esteemed the best. From the latter... a rail-road has been made to the bank of the Kennet and Avon Canal; and by this convenience vast blocks of the stone are put at once on board the barges, and sent up to London, or elsewhere, according to demand*'.

The Quarry was still operating in 1823 – to the dismay of Mr Urban, who wrote to the *Gentleman's Magazine* after a springtime walk over the '*Celtic Vallum*' and enclosure which covers most of the hilltop. He described the Iron Age defences, '*these appear to have been constructed of stone, of which the hill furnished an abundant supply, being one entire rock of freestone*', which he regretted to say '*may in time occasion the disappearance of every trace of this interesting station, quarries having been lately opened within it to some extent*'.[23] His fears were unfounded; although the eastern end of the Iron Age enclosure was obliterated by the workings, they closed before much further damage was done.

The Bathampton Quarries appear to have become run down by September 1829 as Bowsher, by now in his early seventies, gave notice to George Edward Allen that he would '*on the 25th of March next Quit and leave the Possession of the said Quarry lands and Premises*'. He had previously asked for a reduction in rent which was refused and clearly did not wish to pay the higher amount demanded for the outstanding seven years of the lease.

Allen then approached Philip Nowell, a highly successful London Builder, who also owned quarries and a house at Combe Down, hoping that he might take over the lease. Nowell came to inspect the workings and wrote to Allen's agent from the George Inn, Bathampton on 6 March 1830 '*I have been and servayed the Quary on Hampton Down and I find every part of it in such a delapedated state that it really stager me to look on it therefore... I really wish to decline having any thing to do with it*'.[24]

The advertisement of 1836 (see Fig. 74) concerning the building of the second Dry Arch does not make it clear whether or not the Quarries were open at that date. It states that the arch is for '*an intended railroad... from the quarries*'. Does this confirm that the Quarries had closed and the old tramway was derelict? Did Allen insist on the bridge being constructed in case the workings were re-opened and the tramway renovated? If this did not happen the bridge may never have been used for its intended purpose.

BLACK DOG TURNPIKE TRUST.
To *CONTRACTORS, STONE-MASONS,* and
Others.

NOTICE IS HEREBY GIVEN, that the Trustees of the
Black Dog Turnpike Roads will receive Tenders
for building a DRY ARCH for an intended Railroad to lead
from the Stone Quarries of GEORGE EDWARD ALLEN, Esquire,
across the new Turnpike Road, near Bathampton. The Tenders, under seal, directed to " Mr. WM. MC. ADAM, Junr.,
Office of Roads, Bath," must be delivered on or before the
31st day of this Instant March, at the Office of Roads, Saint
James's Parade, Bath ; where the plan and Section of the
Arch and a Specification of the Work to be tendered for may be
seen any day (Saturdays excepted) between the hours of 10
o'clock A M. and 4 o'clock P.M. No Tender will be received
after 12 o'clock at noon on Thursday, the 31st instant.
    ALFRED WHITAKER, Clerk to the Trustees.
Dated Frome, 12th *March,* 1836.

Fig. 74 Advertisement from the *Bath Chronicle*, 24 March 1836.
(By permission of the British Newspaper Archive)

This could have been the case as the Quarries were closed and the tramway derelict by 1847 when Tunstall wrote of the desolation and loneliness of the spot and the rugged path down into the Quarry which was deserted except for the birds singing and the sheep clambering on its *'craggy heights'.* It was a very beautiful place, with *'rugged caves, wild luxuriant trees, creeping plants and fragrant flowers'.* He continued *'the stone from this quarry was conveyed to the Canal by a railroad, which ran down the hill... A few years since, I remember a cottage near the level, of which few traces now remain. The railroad is destroyed and covered with turf.'* He also described a boat trip to Bradford on Avon – when they passed the stone Wharf it was *'now disused, connected with Hampton rocks by the ruined railroad'.*[25]

Fig. 75 The eastern end of the Seven Sisters Quarry – where the
tramway started, c1920. (© Bath in Time – Dafnis Collection)

80

It seems that the Quarries did cease operating in 1829-30. One likely reason is that after the Napoleonic Wars there was a general slump, banks crashed and much building work came to a halt – this badly affected the quarrying industry. It is also possible that the best stone at Bathampton had been worked out. The Quarries probably never re-opened because, prior to the opening of the Great Western Railway in 1841, large quantities of very good quality, easily accessible stone were discovered when Box Tunnel was excavated. Sidings were driven into underground workings providing easy, cheap transportation. Quarries such as those on Combe Down and Hampton Down could not compete on cost or delivery time. The Canal was also badly hit, loosing most of its trade to the railway. The Limpley Stoke Valley was a quieter place after the Quarries closed; the noise from the tramway, as the iron wagon wheels rattled over the joints in the line and the chain ran over its supporting friction sheaves, must have been considerable.

Single Way Mine

After the main area of workings closed a small quarry on the Warren at the Western end of the Down, Single Way Mine, was opened, probably in the mid-1850s.[26] Also known as Single Passage Mine it is located on the Golf Course, about half way between the television masts and Sham Castle, where it provides a hazard for those playing the 18th hole. Stone was taken from this quarry to Bath via a track which ran southwards behind Sham Castle where its course can still be seen. It continued straight on across the parish boundary to join the North Road; this last part, in Bathwick parish, was to the west of the present footpath, and is hardly discernable as it is obscured by woodland and housing.

Fig. 76 Remains of the track above Sham Castle looking south. (G M Huggins, 2013)

In 1855 the owner, Lord William Powlett, leased this last part of the track, which was then 12 feet wide, to Ralph Shuttleworth Allen for 99 years at an annual rent of £5.[27]   Allen, together with his family, servants and the occupiers of his stone quarry on Bathampton Down, was given the right to travel along it with horses, carts, wagons and other carriages, laden or unladen. He had to keep the road with its hedges, fences and ditches, and the gates at either end of this part of the track, with their locks and fastenings, in good repair. Those using it were to shut and lock the gates to ensure that animals grazing on the Down did not escape onto the North Road. The whole length of the track is shown on large scale OS Maps from 1888 to 1932.

The Mine may have closed down towards the end of 1877 as on 22 November an advertisement appeared in the *Bath Chronicle* stating that on the following day, at the Quarry, Bathampton Down, the effects of the lessee, Mr F Hancock, including a crane, iron bars, chains and planks were to be auctioned as he was *'giving up the business'*.[28]

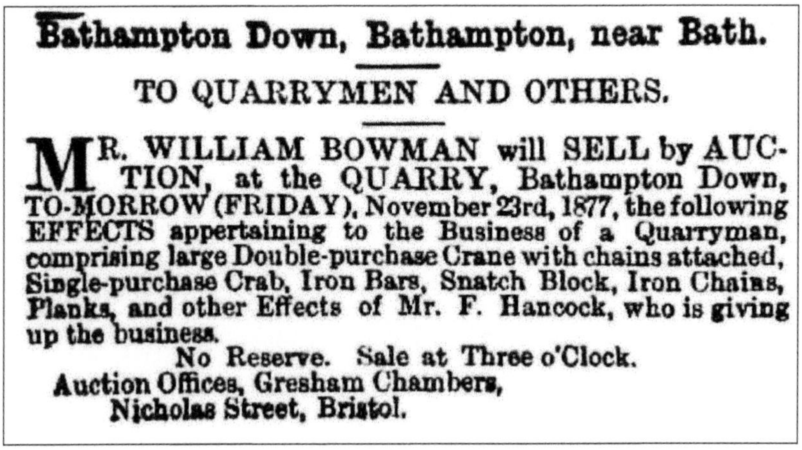

Bathampton Down, Bathampton, near Bath.

TO QUARRYMEN AND OTHERS.

MR. WILLIAM BOWMAN will SELL by AUC-
TION, at the QUARRY, Bathampton Down,
TO-MORROW (FRIDAY), November 23rd, 1877, the following
EFFECTS appertaining to the Business of a Quarryman,
comprising large Double-purchase Crane with chains attached,
Single-purchase Crab, Iron Bars, Snatch Block, Iron Chains,
Planks, and other Effects of Mr. F. Hancock, who is giving
up the business.
        No Reserve. Sale at Three o'Clock.
Auction Offices, Gresham Chambers,
        Nicholas Street, Bristol.

Fig. 77 Advertisement from the *Bath Chronicle,* 22 November 1877.
(By permission of the British Newspaper Archive)

The Quarrymen

Many men must once have worked in the old quarries but there are no records relating to them. Later a very few, who may have worked at Single Way Mine, are listed in the Bathampton Census Returns. One was William Newman, born in the village in 1795. He appears on the first census in 1841, as do Jacob Harrison and his son Daniel. In 1851 only Newman, a Freestone Quarryman living near the George Inn, is listed; similarly in 1861 when he and his family are at the second property in Bathampton Lane (then called St George's Hill). Perhaps he began his working life in the main quarry complex and later obtained employment at Single Way Mine. The track up from St George's Hill would have provided him with an easy route to this quarry on his way to work. He lived to be 75 and died of bronchitis in 1870. His wife Mary-Ann, who was a village laundress, died in 1890 aged 87.

During the 1870s and 80s the census' and local street directories list a Stone Mason Foreman called Jonathan Godwin at Dog's Nose Cottage. There are also four quarrymen – Charles Fell, A Baldwin and James and Joseph Baldwin – who lived in Canal Terrace or Chapel Row at various times. Any of these could have worked at Single Way Mine. There are no quarrymen listed in following census returns.

More recent times

At the height of production the Hampton Rocks area had a bare, rugged, industrial appearance, covered in piles of cut stone, spoil heaps of discarded rubble, trackways and plenty of white stone dust.

Fig. 78 Picnickers on the eastern slopes of Hampton Rocks.
The Devil's Table centre right, c1920. (© Bath in Time – Dafnis Collection)

Photographs from the 1920s show a picturesque scene of caves, rocky outcrops and some scree; the areas between were covered in turf, cropped short by sheep and rabbits which grazed the Down. There are few trees or bushes.

In 1940 fencing was erected to contain tenant Farmer George Candy's sheep which grazed the Golf Course. By 1951 the Club had purchased mowing machinery and the sheep were no longer needed,[29] once the quarry area was not grazed shrubs and trees began to spring up. During the 1950s it was still very open, with far reaching views, but with more vegetation than in the 1920s. Today (2017) the whole area has changed considerably, the once open and rocky slopes below the Quarries are now woodland and there are many trees and bushes in the quarry area, to a great extent obscuring the lovely views. It is hard to find the Devil's Table which has been eroded by the weather and is overgrown.

Fig. 79 The Devil's Table. (G M Huggins, 2012)

All of this area has been used for leisure by local people since the Quarries closed. Walkers have enjoyed the outstanding views, children have scrambled up and down the stony slopes, local scout groups have camped there and families have picnicked, a favourite spot being in the long sheltered 'valley' created by the workings which led to the Seven Sisters at its far end. These were a semi-circle of caves in the cliff face which were the entrances to the old stone mines. They were interconnected at the back by a long cavern which had more workings leading off. It is not known for certain how far these tunnels extended but it is believed locally that you could walk for some distance underground and come out in the Combe Down Quarries.

When Bath was bombed on three successive nights in April 1942 large numbers of people left the City to find shelter in the surrounding hills. Many walked up to Hampton Down, carrying makeshift bedding and their valuables, to spend the nights in the comparative safety of the caves. Some years later, when the Reservoir near to the Seven Sisters was extended in 1954, some of the machinery fell down into old workings below.

There are various unsubstantiated stories of boys being lost in the caves. These may have been told by parents to deter their children from entering as the underground quarries had become an extremely dangerous labyrinth of tunnels with frequent rock falls from the unstable roofs.

Fig. 80 The Netherwood family[30] picnicking at Hampton Rocks, c1905.
(Courtesy of D Netherwood)

By 1961 the Seven Sisters complex was so unsafe that Bath Golf Club, now the landowner, decided to ask the local Territorial Army to seal it off by blowing up the entrances. They had been advised to do so by the convicting magistrate after a homeless man, Laurence Say, was found to be living in the caves and using Single Way Mine as a store for stolen goods.

On the weekend of 4-5 November the soldiers began the work, which provided them with a valuable training exercise.[31] They first blew up three of the cave entrances; tremendous explosions were heard in parts of Bath, houses shook and windows rattled. The Golf Club received a complaint from a lady in Bathampton whose ceiling had cracked and the Committee had to halt the demolition temporarily.

It took the Territorials until the end of the month to complete their task. Although this work was absolutely necessary it completely destroyed an impressive and well known landmark; the long narrow quarry with its picturesque row of large caves was a much loved and visited spot. All that can be seen today are piles of overgrown rubble.

Fig. 81 West end of the Seven Sisters Quarry before demolition, c1920.
(© Bath in Time – Dafnis Collection)

Fig. 82 West end of the Seven Sisters Quarry. (G M Huggins, 2015)

Nevertheless numerous other quarry openings remain. One of these is next to the Devil's Table and is known as the Devil's Cave (ST 76/7775.6519). Some time ago this was explored by cavers who described the isolated pillars of stone left to support the roof. There was a low horizontal tunnel that led for 45 metres to the large main passage which then divided in two. The right hand passage (three metres high and two metres wide) was 60 metres long then branched to the right for another 30 metres. The left hand passage continued for a short distance; after a scramble over rocks there was a confusing maze of passages where a blocked entrance could be seen. The total length of the workings was 300 metres.

Fig. 83 The Devil's Table and Cave, c1920. (© Bath in Time – Dafnis Collection)

They also explored Single Way Mine (ST 76/7700.6516) which was not blown up by the Territorial Army. This had a large tunnel with passages branching off; the entrance being over a pile of collapsed rocks. There was then a boulder slope leading down to a large passage three metres high and two metres wide which ran straight ahead. After passing a short right hand branch it continued for 150 metres, beyond this were complexes of small workings. The total length of this mine was 400 metres.[32]

Fig. 84 The grilled entrance to the North Quarry. (G M Huggins, 2012)

All of the remaining cave entrances are now sealed by metal grills. These prevent the public entering the unsafe workings and provide access and ventilation for the rare bats which hibernate in the caves. It is estimated that 15 per cent of the UK's over wintering population of the Greater Horseshoe Bat inhabits the disused quarries. They are also important hibernation sites for a number of other bat species. The Lesser Horseshoe, Brown Longeared, Natterers, Whiskered and Daubentons have all been regularly recorded and in 1991 the stone mines were designated as a Site of Special Scientific Interest because of the bat population. Nature has now reclaimed the old Quarries.

Fig. 85 Bat Grill at the entrance to the Devil's Quarry.
(Courtesy of David Grosvenor, 2010)

Fig. 86 Greater Horseshoe Bats at Wookey, Somerset. (R F Pickford, 1975)

DEATH OF A VISCOUNT
- a Famous Duel

Among the rich and famous who visited Bath in the autumn of 1778 to take the waters and enjoy the fashionable social scene, were a French nobleman the Viscount Jean Baptiste du Barré, his beautiful young wife (who should not be confused with the Viscount's notorious Aunt, mistress of King Louis XV) and her younger sister.[1] They had rented a house at 8 Royal Crescent which they shared with the Viscount's close friend Count Rice, an Irishman formerly in French military service. Their lifestyle was extravagant with gambling for high stakes, lavish parties and excursions with friends into the surrounding countryside.

On Tuesday 17 November the Viscount was unwell and stayed in his room all day with Count Rice for company. During the evening a dispute arose and a challenge was given; despite much speculation the true cause is still unknown. It has been suggested that the most likely reason was a quarrel over a game of cards – the Viscount already owed Count Rice a great deal of money. Alternatively du Barré may have suspected that his friend was involved with his wife.

At around midnight the Viscount ordered supper, but it was never eaten as the two men, dressed in their greatcoats and accompanied by another Irishman, Mr Toole, stormed out of the house just before one in the morning. The Viscountess, who had been hosting a party, ran out into the Crescent, '*calling after them anxiously*'. She was followed shortly afterwards by the du Barré's valet who found her not far away, '*faint from fear and exhaustion*'. He carried her back to the house then continued to search the streets for his Master and Count Rice but was unable to find them.

Meanwhile the two noblemen had gone to the Three Tuns Tavern in Stall Street, where they hired a coach and four, ostensibly to take them to Bristol. They drove down through the town with their seconds, Toole and a Mr Rogers, and stopped near St James' church at one in the morning to pick up a Bath surgeon, Mr Cadby. When they reached the Old Bridge over the River Avon the postillions were given new orders to drive up to Claverton Down. It is likely that they took the most direct route up nearby Widcombe Hill as at that time Bathwick Hill, although used as a way to the Down, was only a rough narrow track.

To set the scene it may help to describe what the hilltop, which comprised Claverton and Hampton Downs, was like at the time. It was reported to be a '*beautiful extensive level of velvet turf*' with '*peculiarly interesting views*' to the north, south and west.[2] Sham Castle had been built by Ralph Allen sixteen years previously on the western edge of the Downs overlooking Bath. He had also put in a number of plantations of fir trees as can be seen on his Estate Map (see Fig. 23). The turf between these was cropped short by sheep, which were sometimes auctioned off at the nearby Brassknocker Inn.

The Downs were used for all kinds of recreation. Cricket matches were played, horses could be hired for riding and people came by carriage from Bath to enjoy the fresh air and scenery. Near Sham Castle firework parties, sports and bull baiting took place. Until 1792 the original Bath Racecourse (now at Lansdown) was on Claverton Down. It is shown on Thorpe's Map of 1742 and stretched from the Down House (today's Rainbow Wood Farm) north-westerly across to the site of the present Bath University. Race meetings were attended by as many as eight hundred carriages and twenty thousand spectators on foot.

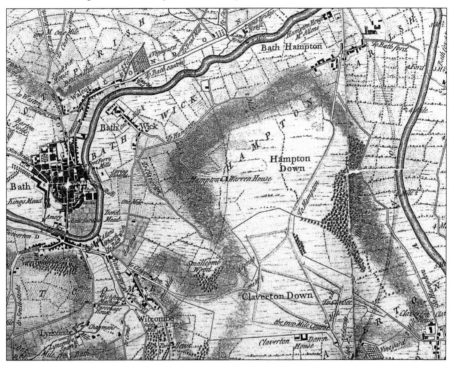

Fig. 87 Extract from Thorpe's *Survey of the City of Bath and five miles around*, 1742. (Bath Record Office)

The Downs could also be lonely and dangerous. A number of reports appeared in the *Bath Chronicle* telling of travellers being held up and robbed and it was known as a place where disputes, such as the one described here, could be settled in private.[3]

The journey to Claverton Down was '*accomplished in moody silence*' and when the coach reached its destination it was about four in the morning of 18 November. The combatants drove around the Down and stopped at the race course grandstand which was probably somewhere near the Down House. They waited in the coach for daylight; during this time du Barré was impatient to get out and proceed with the Duel but was prevented from doing so by the surgeon as it was still extremely dark. Count Rice, by contrast, remained calm and composed. During the wait the seconds, contrary to the rules of duelling, made no attempt to effect reconciliation, indicating that the quarrel was of a serious nature.

When dawn broke soon after six, the two postillions were ordered to drive across the racecourse to the parish boundary wall which separates Claverton from Hampton Down. Du Barré, Rice and their seconds left the coach and 'got over the wall', leaving the surgeon and postillions watching from the Claverton side. They could see the four in conversation about 60 or 70 yards away and heard the firearms being prepared, then watched as the seconds measured out the ground with long paces. The two noblemen took off their coats and, facing each other at a distance of about 25 yards, fired their pistols simultaneously. Count Rice was badly wounded in the groin but limping forward, managed to fire his second pistol, shooting his opponent through the chest. The Viscount fell to the ground and died instantly 'without uttering a word or a groan'. The surgeon ran up but found he could do nothing so went to the assistance of Rice.

Fig. 88 The Duel as illustrated in the *Bath and County Graphic*, July 1897. (BathwickLHS Archive)

Toole removed the Viscount's watch, money and pocket book and then walked back to Bath with Rogers. The surgeon got Rice into the coach and they started to drive across Claverton Down towards the City, having sent the leading postillion to get help. Near the Down House he met three labourers on their way to work and sent them to stay with the body and wait for the Coroner. When he rejoined the coach Count Rice ordered him to go back and collect the weapons (six pistols, three of these had been fired, and two swords) which had been left at the scene.

Just before noon the Viscount's servants came to take care of his body and had it taken down to 'a house in Bathampton'. As the Parish of Bathampton took responsibility for dealing with the death (in accordance with the law of the time) this proves without doubt that the Duel took place on Hampton Down not Claverton Down.

Local tradition has it that the body was laid out and the inquest held at the George Inn. This is likely to be true as rural inquests were often held at the village inn and there are reports of the George being used for such purposes in the 1800s. Members of the public often attended. In the very small, quiet village of Bathampton this inquest was probably one of the most exciting events ever to take place – many people from miles around came to view the corpse. The duel created a sensation not only in the Bath area but nationwide.

The *Bath Chronicle* published a report on the inquest, which was held on Saturday, 21 November, this included the following additional information from the Viscount's valet. He stated that on Tuesday his master and Count Rice had *'appeared cheerful and friendly all day'* however on his last visit to their room at 11.30 in the evening he could see that *'there had been some dispute'*. After the two men left the house he had searched the town for them unsuccessfully and returned home. At nine the next morning Count Rice's servant came with the news that the Viscount *'lay dead on the Down'*.

The jury, composed of twelve or more men from Bathampton, would have had to view the body. They then deliberated for 16 hours and eventually reached a verdict of manslaughter. The inquest report gives the following reasons for their decision:

1) The Viscount's *'implacability and impatience to proceed'*.
2) Two of the three cases of pistols belonged to du Barré.
3) The surgeon stated that the Viscount fired first.
   (This contradicts the report on the Duel which says they fired simultaneously).
4) The seconds were negligent in not persuading the duellists to settle their differences.
5) The code of honour applied in foreign countries, particularly among the military, stated that refusing to accept a challenge to fight would result in disgrace.

By the time the inquest was held Madame du Barré had already left Bath. After her husband's possessions were returned to her she had made a hasty departure for France to escape the gossip and speculation that was rife. Before leaving she instructed the Duke of Northumberland's chaplain to arrange her affairs and organise the funeral. The Viscount's body was duly buried in Bathampton churchyard on Sunday 22 November.

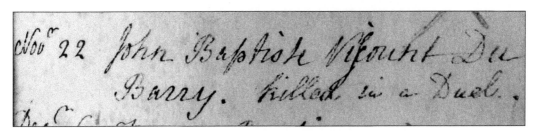

Fig. 89 Entry for 22 November 1778 from the Bathampton Burial Register.
(Somerset Heritage Centre)

A flat rectangular tombstone to the west of the church tower marks his grave.

Fig. 90 The plain flat tombstone marking the grave
of Viscount du Barré. (M F Clark, 2015)

Fig. 91 The inscription on the tombstone. (G M Huggins, 2015)

> *Here rest the Remains*
> *Of*
> *JOHN BAPTISTE, Viscount DU BARRY*
> *Obiit. 18th Novr 1778*

Count Rice eventually recovered from his wound, and was tried at Taunton Assizes on 26 March 1779.[4] In his defence he mentioned the Viscount's impetuous temper and the sums of money du Barré owed him but added, '*It is needless to enter into the origin of that dispute, or impute blame to the deceased, who can no longer vindicate himself.* The judge, after a moving speech in which he noted the defendant's reluctance to fight, directed the jury to bring in a verdict of manslaughter. However, they decided on total acquittal and brought in a verdict of not guilty. Count Rice later returned to the continent where he died in Spain in 1809. Interestingly, an ivory knob said to be from the hilt of his sword is attached to the Bath Town Clerk's Seal and is kept at the Bath Guildhall.

Fig. 92 The Bath Town Clerk's Seal mounted on the hilt from Count Rice's sword.
(M F Clark, 2013)

Fig. 93 Close-up of Seal.
(M F Clark, 2013)

It is said that immediately after the Duel a stone was placed to mark the spot. Over the years many people have searched for this stone and numerous theories put forward as to its position. Not long after the Duel Edmund Rack visited Bathampton between 1781 and 1787 in order to do research for his *Survey of Somerset*. In this book he tells how he rode up to *'the eastern point of the hill called Hampton Cliffs, nearly 700 feet above the river'* where he stood admiring the scenery. He then continues *'About half a mile south of this spot, behind the great plantation of firs which front the city of Bath, the duel was fought... between Count Rice and Count du Barry'*.

James Tunstall's *Rambles around Bath*, published in 1848, also describes the Duel's location. *'At that part of the Down where the Yeomanry were formerly reviewed, a bank slopes towards the wall. It was on the other side of this wall and a few yards from the gate, that the duel took place where a stone slab marks the spot'*.

This fits with the original report of the Duel in the *Bath Chronicle*. The old racecourse ran across Claverton Down to the present University buildings, behind and to the north of these the bank (part of which was once the boundary of the Iron Age enclosure on Hampton Down) slopes upwards. Surmounting this bank is the old wall which still marks the Bathampton/Claverton Parish Boundary. In this is a gateway through which ran an ancient track from Claverton Down to Bathampton. It should be noted however that the original report on the Duel says they *'went over the wall'*, not through a gate. Some distance to the west of the gateway there is a large upright stone slab set into the wall which is an old stile (see Fig. 95 below and Figs 196-7) – does this explain the above comment?

Fig. 94 The remains of the ancient track where it passes southwards through the gateway: the rest of its route was obliterated when the University was built and the right of way diverted. (M F Clark, 2013)

Fig. 95 The stone slab once set in the wall which has now been breached to allow the diverted bridleway to pass through (looking north). (M F Clark, 2013)

A discussion in the *Bath Chronicle* of 1935 talked of local people who remembered '*a stone with initials and a date*', but said that despite extensive searching the stone could no longer be found.[5]   More recent correspondence[6] has suggested that there was a large rectangular slab in the vicinity of the nearby reservoir until 2006 when it was accidentally damaged and removed.

The exact spot where the fatal confrontation took place will never be known but it can be pinned down to a fairly small area. During the early 1780s, according to Rack's description, Ralph Allen's 'Fir Forest', behind Sham Castle, was still in existence.[7] This covered the entire western end of the Warren behind the Wall which divided the Down (see Fig. 5) and would have provided a very secluded spot for a Duel. It also narrows down the possible site to a fairly level stretch of land on the southern edge of the present Bath Golf Course, about 70 yards inside the Bathampton Parish boundary wall. Du Barré and Rice must have fought somewhere in the vicinity of what is now the ninth fairway, between the gate to the east and the Wall which divided the Down to the west, a short part of which was rebuilt in 2016.

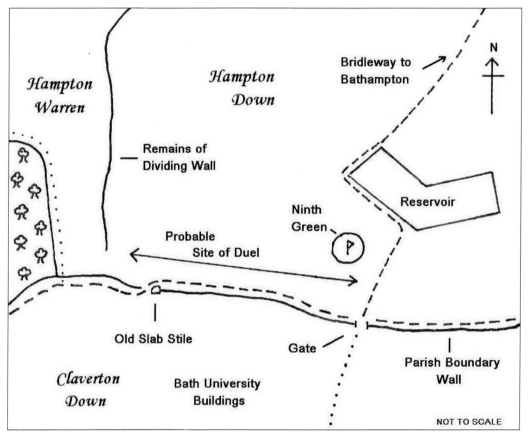

Fig. 96 Plan of the southern edge of the Bath Golf Club Course
showing the approximate site of the Duel. (M F Clark, 2015)

Needless to say the story of the Duel and the stone which marked the spot has been passed down through local families for generations and the following poem (which appeared in the *Bath and County Graphic* of July 1897) is an example of how it has formed part of local folklore.

A November Night, 1778

1.

Jean du Barry is gay to-night,
  And open house he keeps,
With mirth and music and laughter light,
  While the sober city sleeps.
With a winsome wife and a friend right true,
  And of wealth a goodly store,
The roses of life his pathway strew,
  What can he wish for more?

2.

Jean du Barry was gay to-night,
  Was gay but an hour ago;
But his brow is gloomy, his lips are white
  As he paces to and fro.
And why does this wife he holds so dear
  Falter amid the dance?
And why should the friend to his heart so near
  Turn from his troubled glance?

3.

Perchance 'twas the low-toned talk o'erheard
  As unseen by a door he stood;
Pity it is that a whispered word
  Should have changed his mirthful mood!
Madame is smiling and dancing still,
  Maybe, 'neath the crimson rose
That nods on her breast, her heart grows chill
  As she wonders "how much he knows!"

4.

Jean du Barry will play tonight,
  Will play, though the stakes are high,
And he wins and wins the guineas bright,
  But no gladness lights his eye.
"Luck at cards – you know the rest,"
  Quoth his friend with a taunting look,
"Much thanks my lord! 'Tis a stale old jest,
  And one I scarce can brook."

5.

"Your meaning, Sir?" "Tis a false, false game,"
  Cries Jean below his breath,
"But what need to blazon the woman's name
  When two men fight 'till death?"
"I take you, Sir! At dawn we meet."
  "Where, how, and when you will!"
The music rings out shrill and sweet,
  And Madame is dancing still!

A November Morn, 1778

6.

The mist hangs low over Claverton Down,
  The morning is dull and grey,
'Tis a weary climb from the distant town,
  In the first chill hours of day.
But some were here ere the first, faint gleam
  From the tardy, wintry sun,
They have fled like phantom forms in a dream,
  But they left behind them one.

7.

And the timid hare with startled eyes
  O'er the trampled grass flits by,
Fearing the form that silent lies
  With still face turned to the sky.
There is none to mourn, there is none to tend,
  On the ground with his life blood red,
Slain by his own familiar friend,
  Lies Jean du Barry – dead.

F. T.

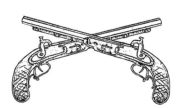

97

THE RIFLE RANGE

From 1860 until 1894 there was a Rifle Range on Hampton Down used for target practice and competition shooting by the Volunteer Militia, a type of Home Guard which had been in existence for many years. Its numbers increased dramatically during the Napoleonic and Crimean Wars but fell again afterwards; as a result more recruits were needed when there was a renewed threat of invasion from France in 1858. Men from every walk of life joined up and became interested in rifle shooting and marksmanship. The threat soon receded but the Government felt that a national support defence force was still necessary especially as it gave a sense of duty, national pride and self discipline to young men from labouring communities.

On 19 January 1860 'A Rifleman' wrote to the *Bath Chronicle* that '*The Rifle Movement is daily gaining ground in country districts, and during the past fortnight the villages of Bathampton, Bathford, Claverton, Limpley Stoke and Freshford have united, and it is expected will shortly be formed into a Corps*'. He admired the '*alacrity*' with which the men came forward but deplored their wish to keep their rifles at home, '*in the name of order and safety, who would place rifles in the hands of the community and why should raw countrymen be allowed, when not on duty, to ... carry about such dangerous weapons?*'

Despite these fears the 1st Battalion of the 45th Somerset Rifle Volunteers was raised at Bath later that year, having seven Corps gathered from the surrounding district. These included the 14th Corps, known locally as the Warleigh Manor Rifle Volunteers, who recruited along the Avon Valley from Freshford to Bathampton. It was founded by Henry Duncan Skrine of Warleigh Manor, Bathford (born c1815, died 1901) and continued by his son Henry Mills Skrine (born 1844, died 1915). The Somerset Rifle Volunteers lasted until 1882 when they became the 1st Volunteer Battalion, Prince Albert's 4th Somerset Light Infantry, which was later amalgamated into the Territorial Army when it was set up in 1908.

Fig. 97 (Above right) Col. Henry Duncan Skrine.

Fig. 98 (Right) Col. Henry Mills Skrine.
From the *Bath & County Graphic*,
1897 and 1898. (Bathwick LHS Archive)

Joining up was not cheap for the working man. There was an initial outlay of £3 12s 6d for the uniform and a cost of £4 10s 0d for the rifle, although the latter could be paid for out of Corps funds. Despite this, rifle shooting became very popular and soon developed into serious competition with the National Rifle Association being founded in 1860. In that year the Volunteers set up the Hampton Down Rifle Range running west to east on a long, fairly level, stretch of land now the 5th and 6th holes of the Bath Golf Club Course, situated below the top escarpment on the northern side of the Down above Bathampton village. The targets were placed at the east end of the Range in front of the Butts, a stone embankment which can still be seen and is part of the former quarries. There were firing points on Hampton Down at 200, 250, 300 and 400 yards. Two more were sited on the Warren at 500 and 600 yards – as the dividing wall was still in existence the riflemen using these had to fire over it at the targets. For long distance practice a 1,000 yard range was constructed at Warleigh in 1869.

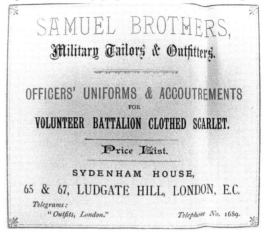

Fig. 99 Samuel Brothers Advert for Military Tailoring. nd. (Somerset Heritage Centre)

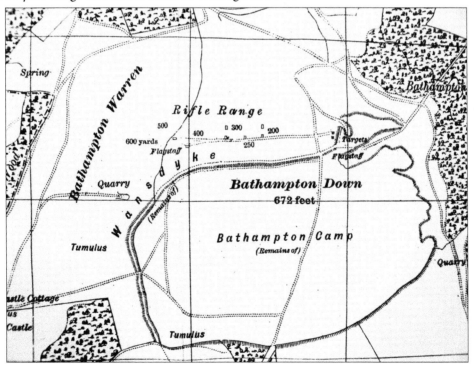

Fig. 100 From Houlston's undated Plan of Bath – based on the first OS Map dated 1882, looking north. Clearly showing how the Rifle Range crossed the dividing wall between the Warren and Hampton Down. (Bath Record Office)

The first of many reports of shooting competitions at Hampton Down appeared in the *Bath Chronicle* of the 5 November 1860. It was held between the four Bath Corps (Bath, Bathwick, Lyncombe and Walcot) on this occasion there was prize money totalling £10 but often the winner was presented with an ornate, engraved silver spoon similar to the one illustrated in Fig. 101 (below). This was awarded to Sgt F J R Urch of the Volunteers and the Territorials. Hallmarked 1909, it is initialled NRA (National Rifle Association) on the reverse, Fig. 102 (below).

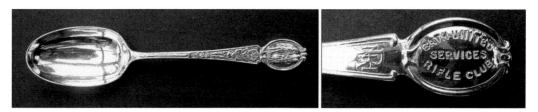

Figs. 101 and 102 (M F Clark, 2014)

The spent lead shot left after firing provided a lucrative source of income for petty thieves and in July 1862 a boy named John Frost was fined two shillings for causing wilful damage to the Butts. Such thefts had become a major problem nationwide so an Act of Parliament was passed for better protection of rifle butts, carrying a full penalty of £5. This does not seem to have been a sufficient deterrent as in August John Clark was also summonsed for damaging the Rifle Butts at Bathampton. Charles Perkins, Keeper of the Butts, gave evidence – he had seen the defendant with another man searching for bullets having '*cut out two large pieces of turf for that purpose*'. Clark was fined £1 or 21 days hard labour as he had a previous caution.

When John Hampton was prosecuted by the Volunteers ten years later Perkins said that a '*deal of damage had been done to the Butts by people searching for lead*'.

As a result shooting practice had to cease while they were repaired; sometimes it took two men a week to put right.

On the 23 January 1872, when he saw Hampton and three others beating the Butts with sticks and an iron bar, he gave chase and caught Hampton who had six and a half pounds of lead on

Fig. 103 Lead shot from the Butts.
(G M Huggins, 2014)

him. Despite claiming that he was not there, it was his brother, the defendant was committed to gaol for 14 days. Remnants of spent shot can still be found by those with a keen eye.

During April 1886 Colonel Henry Skrine, Commander of the Volunteers, received a letter informing him that a three year old mare, valued at £35, belonging to Farmer Candy of Bathampton, had died as a result of being shot while grazing on part of the Range about 400 yards from the targets. The carcase was examined by a vet who confirmed that the horse had died as the result of a gunshot although no bullet was found.

On 30 April a Court of Enquiry was held at Bath by the Volunteers who maintained that there had been no rifle practice on the Range at the time the mare was injured; there was also evidence that a lone unauthorised marksman had been on the Down using a revolver. It was impossible to show whether the wound was caused by a bullet from a revolver or one of the Martine Rifles used by the soldiers. In these circumstances the Court decided that the Volunteers should pay Mr Candy £20 to compensate him for his loss if, on his part, he exonerated them from all blame.

The safety of those using the Down became an increasing concern. At a Bath Golf Club meeting on 2 March 1893 the secretary mentioned the risk to golfers from the Rifle Range in view of the nine holes being made to expand the course (which had opened in 1881) to 18 holes. A letter was sent to Colonel Skrine expressing the Club's concern, especially about the danger of ricochets from the embankment behind the targets. The Colonel, however, felt that the Range could be used '*without undue risk*', although it was impossible to make it absolutely safe. It had been used for 30 years without accident and the troops had previous training in firing at HQ.

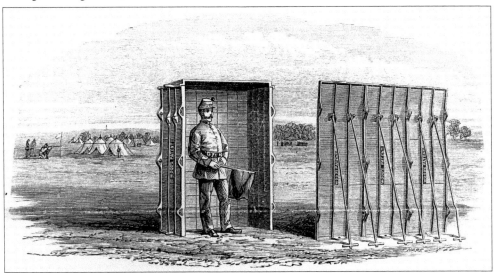

Fig. 104 Advert from Woods 'Universal' Targets, nd. (Somerset Heritage Centre)

More complaints were made by the Great Western Railway about ammunition falling on their Weymouth Line. In summer bullets had been picked up on the Warleigh side of the river and men working on the Bradford Road (A363) had been forced to leave work on one occasion for their own safety. The Volunteers placed a Sergeant '*on the South side of the hill*' to check this and he reported that several bullets passed over '*the Quarry in which the murder took place and at that time a good many people were visiting it'*. This refers to Elsie Luke whose remains were discovered in September 1893, see pages 103-119.

Fig. 105 Hampton Rocks above the Avon Valley looking south-east towards Warleigh, c1886 – near the quarry where Elsie Luke's body was to be found a few years later.
(W Mannings – Harbutt Collection)

It became obvious that nothing could be done to make the Range safe and in June 1894 the Volunteers gave six months notice of intention to vacate. The landowner, Ralph Edward Allen of Bathampton Manor, was probably greatly relieved as in February of that year he too had written to the Colonel saying he regarded the Range as unsafe and was glad there had been no serious accident. As a result the Hampton Down Range closed and for a time the soldiers used one at Brislington but this was too far away to be convenient. In October 1896, however, the 1st Volunteer Battalion's Annual Return states that *'Musketry returns show considerable improvement, greatly due to practice at the New Range at Box,* [commissioned in 1880] *which is most satisfactory'*.

THE HAMPTON ROCKS MYSTERY
- the life and death of Elsie Luke

In Bathampton churchyard, to the north-west of the church tower, stands a tall plain headstone with a poignant yet intriguing inscription – 'Here lie the remains of ELSIE ADELINE LUKE, aged 26, who was cruelly murdered on Hampton Down, August 1891', and at the bottom of the stone, 'This replacement stone was funded by the estate of Lucy Barlow'. Many people have asked, "Who was Elsie, was she connected with Bathampton, what happened to her, and why did the Barlow estate replace her headstone?"

Fig. 106 The Headstone in Bathampton churchyard.
(M F Clark, 2013)

Elizabeth, or Elsie as she was usually referred to, was not a Bathampton girl. She was born in London in about 1867, the last of four children of James and Elizabeth Luke, who had come to join the German immigrant population in the East End. Tracing her family is difficult as the East Enders liked to keep a low profile; births, marriages and deaths often went unregistered. Her father probably died while she was a small child as by the 1881 census her mother is shown as the wife of Frederick Wilke, a bootmaker from Cologne, with whom she had four more children.

The family was poor and by the age of 14 Elsie was in trouble. She appeared at the Thames Magistrates Court on 12 April 1880, as Elizabeth Luke or Wilke, charged with *'felony in service'*. Mr Lushington, the magistrate, sent her to prison for 10 days and then to the Limpley Stoke Reformatory for 5 years. Such Reformatories were introduced to provide training and a better environment for poor children who had offended. It was hoped to improve their behaviour and character, and by teaching the girls housework, laundry and needlework, to fit them for a life of domestic service.

Fig. 107 The Limpley Stoke Reformatory, 1910. (www.freshford.com)

The Limpley Stoke Reformatory opened in 1861. Philip Charles Sheppard, a local magistrate and educationalist who lived at Bathampton Manor, was on the organizing committee and became the first manager, supported by a matron. The first inspection report was unsatisfactory and after a year he handed over the running of the Reformatory to his wife Mary, who improved things greatly. By 1875 the Sheppards had moved from Bathampton to Waterhouse, near Limpley Stoke and by 1890 their eldest unmarried daughter, Elizabeth, had taken over as superintendent. Miss Rodman, Matron during Elsie's time at Limpley Stoke, found Elsie to be good looking, healthy, a hard worker with nice manners, quick, intelligent and good at lessons. Unfortunately she had a violent temper and at times Matron had to lock her in her room to calm down with some sewing – she was an excellent seamstress. In 1881 Elsie was confirmed at Winsley Church where the girls attended service clad in blue dresses and red cloaks.

She left the Reformatory on 3 May 1885, aged 19. The Matron *'could not send this poor thing out'* into service because of her temper so she returned to her mother in Plaistow, London, where she worked as a dressmaker. Matron visited Elsie there as did Fanny Spratt, the kindly Head Laundress, who had been in charge of her. Elsie did not get on well at home as her stepfather struck her, and wrote to Matron saying she was returning to Bath. She also wrote to Fanny, who had left her job at the Reformatory when she married John Bowles of nearby Turleigh, saying she was in great distress and had been ordered into the country as she suffered from epileptic fits. Mrs Bowles sent her 2s 6d for the train fare. Elsie found lodgings in Bath and made a scant living taking in needlework. She often walked out to see Mrs Bowles who would give her a meal, some employment and help with her rent, and continued to treat her kindly despite finding her far from truthful, bad tempered and tiresome.

During the spring of 1890 Elsie met Arthur Coombs, an apprentice with Fuller's Carriage Works in Bath, who was only seventeen but looked older. They '*walked out*' together about three times a week and often went to the Railway Mission Hall in Monmouth Street, although Elsie was disliked there.

In that year Elsie found employment at Dean's Irish Linen Warehouse in Northgate Street, but had to leave as she was subject to fainting fits; she then worked for several different employers as a domestic servant.

Fig. 108 Elsie in her maid's uniform, c1891. (Courtesy of M Harris)

Later she found a position at Clifton, near Bristol. While she was there Arthur found out about her past and that she had lied to him about her family, pretending that her stepfather was Superintendent of an emigrants home where he supposedly earned a large salary. Because of all this and because his parents disapproved of her, Arthur wrote to Elsie to break off the relationship. Shortly afterwards he began seeing Mary Louisa Sheppard (known as Polly). Elsie, who had left her job in Clifton and returned to Bath, became extremely jealous and went to great lengths to get Arthur back. One dark night in February 1891 she was seen outside 25 Kingsmead Terrace, Arthur's home, crying and banging on the door. When his father eventually let her in she said she was pregnant, Arthur having 'taken liberties' with her in Victoria Park at Christmas. The young man angrily denied this and Mr Coombs got Elsie to leave by saying they 'would see what happened'. She never returned and Arthur became engaged to Polly in March.

During that month Elsie stayed with Miss Hull (formerly the needlework mistress at the Reformatory) at 7 Kingsmead Buildings. On the 21 March she registered with an employment agency, giving a false reference, and was soon found work as a cook with Mr and Mrs J Kerry of Cheriton House, Oldfield Park. This large house, now a hotel, was a suitably impressive residence for James Kerry who was Director and Secretary of Colmers, a well known Bath department store. The 1891 census, taken on 5 April, shows Elise A Luke [sic] and another servant at Cheriton House with the Kerrys and their six children.

The family found Elsie to be well spoken, well conducted in the house, able to speak some French and read music, but she had a quick temper. She was 'superior looking and superior in her manner too', short and slight, with nice neat teeth and wore a gold watch and chain. Sometimes she went into the garden for air as she felt faint. Once again Elsie lied, telling them that she had come to Bath to nurse her sick mother and that Mr and Mrs Bowles of Turleigh were her Uncle and Aunt.

Elsie's next ploy was to send Polly a bundle of love letters which Arthur had written her; these Polly burnt. In February 1891 Polly wrote Arthur the first of 161 letters, many of these referred to Elsie. In them she called her 'a beast of a girl' and said her claim of pregnancy was untrue – she was just trying to get Arthur back. She begged Arthur not to have anything to do with Elsie, and stated that her attendance at the Mission was 'a mockery, if she thinks she is going to mar our happiness she is mistaken' and 'she can faint when she likes'. Whenever Elsie saw Polly in the street she would shout at her and once hit her, but Polly wrote, 'I'm not afraid of her'. In short, Elsie caused as much trouble for the young couple as possible in an attempt to break them up.

Arthur may still have been seeing Elsie as Kate Bullock, a fellow servant at Cheriton House, saw a young man who visited in the evenings when Elsie would take him down into the cellar. He was short, thin and fair, with a light complexion and was 19 or 20; the same age as Arthur, who was of medium height, thin and pale, with a large square face, staring eyes, prominent upper lip, protruding teeth, and a mass of curly light brown hair.

Fig. 109 Sketch of Arthur Coombs, *Bath Chronicle*, 5 October 1893.
(Reproduced by kind permission of the British Newspaper Archive)

It seems that Elsie was still convinced that Arthur loved her despite his engagement. On the second Sunday in July she told a neighbour, James Robertson, that she had made it up with him and they were to be married in two or three weeks time, when he would leave home without telling his parents. At about the same time Mr Kerry gave Elsie notice as *'he did not like her acquaintances'*. He thought she left on July 31 but his wife was certain that it was on Saturday 25 as on that day she asked for the sovereign that was due to her in wages, saying that she was going to London as an Uncle had died and left her some money – another untruth. She was expected back on Monday evening to work out her notice but never returned. Afterwards Mrs Kerry found that some clothing was missing – a new dress, a nightdress, and some underwear. Kate Bullock had seen Elsie hand two bundles over the garden wall to a young girl standing in Cedar Walk, just before she left at 4pm on Saturday carrying a small parcel. She said she was not coming back and would sleep at Kingsmead Street that night.

During July Elsie had been to Oliver's Boot Shop in Westgate Street, where she persuaded the manager, George Malpas, to supply her with a smart pair of Oxford Boots, without taking payment, by saying she was purchasing them for Mrs Kerry. He never got his money as when he called at Cheriton House he was told that Elsie had gone.

On the morning of Sunday 26 July 1891 two young men, Arthur Clare and Alfred Phillips, were sitting on the branch of a tree overhanging the St George's Hill Track, which leads from the Warminster Road through Fussells Wood to Hampton Down, where they had fixed up a trapeze so that they could train for the sports on Bank Holiday Monday 3 August. They saw

Arthur Coombs and Elsie walking up the track together, '*they were bound to pass under the bough to go through the gate*' at the top. It seems unlikely that they were mistaken as Clare had met Elsie when she stayed with his Aunt, Miss Hull, and both had been to school with Coombs.

Fig. 110 Gate leading to St George's Hill Track viewed from
Hampton Down, c1896. (W Mannings – Harbutt Collection)

If Mrs Kerry was correct in thinking that Elsie left Cheriton House on 25 July there is a gap of about a week when it is not known where she was staying, but during that week she called on her friend Lucy Isaacs at Calton Road to collect a photograph of herself. She told her she was leaving on Bank Holiday Monday to marry Arthur but did not say where they were going. Lucy had known her for two or three years, since they were in service together at Mr Dykes in Norfolk Crescent, and did not believe her as she had heard the same story many times and had '*found her out in many lies before*'. Elsie did not say she was pregnant or appear to be so.

On Saturday 1 August Elsie called on another friend, Mrs Annie Hayman of 11 Kingsmead Terrace, asking if she could sleep at her house until Tuesday morning as the Kerrys were away and she had just seen them off at the GWR station – a complete fabrication. Mrs Hayman suggested she tried Mrs Harriet Dillon at number 26 (the Coombs family were at number 25). Elsie seemed depressed and told Mrs Hayman that she had been engaged to Arthur for some time and was three months pregnant with his child; she seemed less bright than usual but not suicidal. At 3pm she knocked on Mrs Dillon's door and obtained lodgings which she said Mrs Kerry would pay for. She appeared highly respectable and wore a black straw hat. (It may have been Mrs Dillon's daughter who took the bundles of clothing over the wall). The next day, Sunday 2, Annie Poole of number 27 saw Elsie sitting in Mrs Dillon's garden reading, dressed in a white apron and cuffs. In the afternoon she saw her go down the steps at the bottom of the terrace, followed shortly afterwards by Arthur Coombs. Mrs Hayman also saw Elsie twice that day, in the morning when Elsie paid her a visit, and in the afternoon talking to Arthur.

Elsie left Mrs Dillon's at 10.30 on the morning of Monday 3 August 1891 (Bank Holiday) saying she was going to Turleigh for the day, however Mrs Bowles was adamant that she did not arrive there. Perhaps she went to the Reformatory instead as the Matron saw her for the last time that weekend; she had come to say '*Goodbye*' as she was returning to London. Mrs Dillon did not see Elsie again; she had left behind an old black dress, a mirror and a nightgown marked with Mrs Kerry's initials. As Elsie had not returned by Tuesday she assumed she had gone back to the Kerrys' and returned the gown to Cheriton House.

Mrs Hayman saw Elsie twice on Bank Holiday Monday, in the morning when she said she was going to Turleigh by train and again at 5pm talking to a woman at the bottom of the terrace. Elsie then walked alone alongside the river towards the GWR, wearing her black straw hat. This was the last time she was seen alive.

Fig. 111 Sketch of Elsie Luke, *Bath Chronicle*, 5 October 1893.
(Reproduced by kind permission of the British Newspaper Archive)

About an hour later, Arthur Clark aged 15, and his brother Frank, 13, were with a party having a picnic at Hampton Rocks when they saw an agitated young man wearing only his shirt and socks. He told them his clothes had been stolen while he was swimming in the Avon, which they thought very strange as the river was a mile away. He said he would go home once it was dark, and when they left at 7pm they saw him again in a wood near the quarries. He had a moustache so was not Arthur Coombs who was clean shaven. On Friday 7 August Frank Clark was on the Downs again when he found a lady's hat, made of black open work straw, trimmed with black and cream, near Claverton Woods. He took it to Bath Police Station where they recorded the find.

The Bath Volunteers, who used the Rifle Range next to Hampton Rocks, were at camp in Devizes that week so the Down was less frequented than usual. Arthur Coombs was a Volunteer but did not go as he had to help his father. William Henry Dill, of Lower Weston, marker for the Volunteers at the Rifle Butts, did attend the camp, and resumed his usual duties after they returned. He occasionally slept in a hut on the Down because shooting often went on until dusk and he could not pick up the spent cartridges until first thing next morning. He had known the Downs for forty years and often walked round to see what he could find. He was on duty on August 12 and 13 and on one of those days, when he went for his usual early morning walk, picked up a cuff saturated with blood and a lady's gold watch and chain, about four feet from the edge of a small quarry. The watch appeared to have been wrenched off as it was broken. He took these items back to the butts and showed the cuff to the Assistant Marker, Frederick Field. He kept quiet about the watch and chain, hoping to claim a reward for finding them. The two men returned to the quarry and, looking over the edge, saw the other cuff. They scrambled down and 'beat about the nettles' where, a few feet from the entrance to a small cavern, they found a lady's handkerchief, similarly blood stained and marked with the name A H Kerry. Quite unaccountably Dill did not consider his finds suspicious as 'he had found lots of strange things up there'. He did, however, show the cuffs and handkerchief to two policemen at the markers' hut, which was a point where the constables of the County Constabulary met. These he kept but sold the watch chain. Early in 1892 he raffled the watch, which he claimed his sister had given him, at the Exeter Inn in Southgate Street. The landlord won it for his daughter Mrs Harding, wife of a Limpley Stoke farmer.

Two years had passed since Elsie was last seen on that Bank Holiday Monday when, on the morning of Friday 22 September 1893, two 12 year old Bath College boys, Cecil Brand and Alex Emerson, made a gruesome discovery. They set out, armed with a candle, to explore the caves of the disused quarry workings at Hampton Rocks and scrambled down the 15 foot drop into a small quarry at the eastern end of Hampton Down, near the wall which forms the parish boundary between Bathampton and Claverton. While playing there they went into a small cavern on the north side of the old working (OS ST 778.651). By the light of their candle and aided by some natural light in the cave Alex Emerson saw a bone; he lifted a stone and found a skull and some shoes still on the feet of a skeleton. The boys went straight to Cecil's home on Bathwick Hill and told his father, Captain Brand, who returned to the cave that day with PC Wall of Bath City Police.

The case, however, had to be dealt with by the County Constabulary as the remains were found in Bathampton, outside Bath City boundary. Police from two adjoining parishes had to attend as Bathampton had no constable of its own at that time. On the following morning, the Constable took Police Sgt Edwards of Batheaston, PC Brunt of Bathford and two reporters to the cavern.

Fig. 112 The quarry face on which a cross and inscription were carved - fallen debris now covers the cave entrance. (G M Huggins, 2012)

The cave was secluded with two openings, only one large enough for an adult to enter. This was low down in the ground, only 1½ feet deep and 4 feet wide and partly concealed by a large stone, making entry difficult. Sgt Edwards managed to crawl in feet first and found a cave 20 feet long, 12 feet wide and 3½ feet high, the uneven floor sloped down slightly and was of loose stone. At once he saw a leg bone and shoe protruding from a pile of large stones covering the skeleton – the body had been dragged in feet first and lay face down, the left leg drawn up over the right thigh. The scraps of clothing clinging to the dry bones were almost unrecognisable, but some corsets were well preserved and parts of a wire bustle remained. A pair of almost new Oxford shoes was still good – no money or jewellery was found. Most of a plaited coil of light brown hair had been eaten by rodents and it was clear from the fractured skull that there had been a severe blow to the left temple. It took the police less than an hour to collect the remains carefully and put them in a sack. This was carried to the George Inn at Bathampton where they were laid out on a table in an outhouse to await the Surgeon's examination and the Coroner's Inquest.

On Monday 25 September Mr Charles Harper, Surgeon of Bathford, examined the remains which were reduced to a skeleton apart from the feet which had been protected by the shoes. His opinion was that they were those of a young woman aged 19 to 21, five feet tall, who was slight and had perfect teeth. The right foot was dislocated with the toes drawn up. The fingers were also contracted showing that she died in convulsions, consistent with a fractured skull causing death. The one inch square fracture on the left frontal lobe had occurred before death and was due to a violent blow. Some portions of underwear had survived including part of a pair of drawers marked A H Kerry. That same day the first

111

newspaper reports on the 'supposed murder' were printed and Dill realised the significance of his finds; he handed the cuffs and handkerchief in to the police and told them about the watch and chain. Superintendent Rutherford and Detective Sgt Smith were put in charge of the case; they viewed the remains and began their enquiries.

On Tuesday the Coroner for North Somerset, Mr Samuel Craddock, opened the inquest at the George, the jury of fifteen men having viewed the cave and the remains beforehand. The foreman of the jury was Henry Dolman, aged 52, of Canal Terrace, Bathampton; landlord of the George which was managed by his son Thomas.

Fig. 113 Henry Dolman, c1910, former Landlord of The George Inn.
(Courtesy of Pauline Lowes)

Cecil Brand and Sgt Edwards described the cavern and finding the body, then Dill was questioned. He insisted that he had shown his finds to PC Brunt at the time but the constable denied this. The Surgeon gave his report – he believed something 'had happened on the top' and the body was thrown into the quarry. The remains had been there for a considerable time; he 'could not say how long, it depended on the number of rodents about'. A juryman commented that 'the place swarmed with stoats' and Henry Dolman interrupted with 'it is very evident that it was a foul murder'.

The Coroner adjourned the inquest; he then instructed the police to photograph the cave and its surroundings and issued a certificate for the burial of 'a certain woman' to take place at the expense of the parish. Shortly afterwards the name Kerry on the clothing led to the remains being identified as those of Elsie Luke (or Wilkie) whose description closely matched the Surgeon's report, so burial was deferred.

At about this time Elsie's name and a cross were roughly carved on the rock face above the cave, which became known locally as 'The Murder Hole'. It is still just possible to make out the cross and inscription but it must be emphasised that the climb down is difficult, the cave no longer accessible and the quarry itself dangerous, being littered with loose rocks and fallen trees.

Figs. 114 and 115 The cross and remains of the inscription in 2005.
(BLHRG, A H Green Collection)

The murder caused intense interest and by the next weekend people were arriving at the site by 6am to search for the money Elsie had on her. On Sunday 1 October thousands of sightseers came and vendors of ginger beer and apples were doing a profitable trade at the Rocks. It was just like a fair and many were tricked into buying sheep's bones purporting to be part of the skeleton. Interest continued for some time and the Volunteers became concerned that, because of the number of people on the Down, someone might get hit by a stray bullet. Some even had souvenir photographs taken as in the following illustration which shows two young men sitting above the entrance to the cavern with the cross to the left of them.

Fig. 116 Two unidentified young men at the cave, c1893. The cross can be seen left of centre.
(Courtesy of M Harris)

Suspicion soon fell on Arthur Coombs and on 28 September he was arrested at work, the next day he appeared at Weston Police Court charged with the murder of his former sweetheart during August 1891. He denied the charge but seemed agitated and nervous. Mr E B Titley represented him and Mr Canning Collins, a Bath solicitor, acted for the prosecution.

The police described removing the remains from the cave and their unsuccessful search for the jewellery and money which Elsie had when she disappeared. They had recovered the watch from Mrs Harding at her cottage near the Viaduct Inn and the blood stained items from Dill, who was too drunk to be called. They were unable to trace Elsie's relatives in London. Margaret Ann Kerry spoke of Elsie's temperamental character, fainting fits and dismissal and identified the linen and handkerchief as being some of the stolen items. After several months she had opened a box which Elsie left behind; it contained two old dresses and some letters which she burnt without reading.

The Matron from the Reformatory explained Elsie's background and said she had last seen her on the Saturday before Bank Holiday. Other witnesses told of her friendship with Arthur and how they had gone to the Mission Hall together. John Edwards, a fishmonger of James Street West, remembered Arthur saying that Elsie *'ought to be dead or killed'*. Mrs Hayman and Mrs Dillon gave evidence that Elsie stayed in Kingsmead Terrace before she was last seen at 5pm on Bank Holiday Monday. Lastly Lewis Vigus, a Bath chemist, told how Arthur came to his shop on the Wednesday or Thursday after Bank Holiday when he had treated his hand which was so severely injured that he was unable to work.

There followed three more Magisterial Hearings – the last being on 17 October. Between these Arthur was held on remand at Horfield Prison in Bristol. On each occasion crowds waited for him to arrive at Weston Railway Station and the gates of the courthouse were besieged by people trying to get in.

Mr Collins was keen to prove that Arthur had a motive for murder. He produced Polly's letters to Arthur, many of which referred to the problems the young couple were having with Elsie – significantly there was a gap in the letters between July 22 and August 13 1891. He also called witnesses to prove that Arthur was seeing both girls at the same time and contended that Arthur's injury, a human bite to the thumb, could have been caused during the struggle above the quarry. A broken silver brooch of Elsie's had also been found at Arthur's house. '*A man who was entangled with two women*', said Mr Collins, '*might want to get rid of one of them*'.

As the hearing progressed it became apparent that much of the evidence heard was vague and contradictory and Mr Titley proved that Arthur's injury had occurred during a fight after the Liberal Fête on 27 July, a week before the murder took place. At this point Mr Collins stated that there was no need to call more witnesses; there was insufficient evidence to send Coombs for trial. Should they do so and he was found not guilty he could not be tried again if further evidence came to light, but if the case was closed now it could be reopened later. The Magistrates, however, wished to question Polly Sheppard. At first she had been uncommunicative but now said that her letters referred to her jealousy of Miss Thorne, a cousin of Arthur's whom he had been showing around the area – she had seen less of him as a result and '*a coldness*' had grown up between them. She then provided Arthur with an alibi for the evening of Bank Holiday; he had collected her at about 5pm, they had gone for a short walk and then to the theatre to see 'The Dancing Girl'. Her employer, she said, had seen them there.

The Magistrates soon reached a verdict. There was a strong case of suspicion against Coombs but not sufficient evidence to convict him so they could not restrain him any longer. The case was dismissed to deafening cheers in court and Arthur embraced his father and shook him by the hand.

Meanwhile the inquest had been running concurrently with the court case. In all it sat for seven sessions, most were at the Parish Rooms in Bathampton High Street but the last, on 6 December 1893, was held at the George Inn as the Rooms were under repair. Much the same evidence was produced as at the Magistrates' Hearing. Mr Titley tried to prove that Elsie had had another boyfriend, Henry Bevan of Plaistow, who once visited her in Bath, and to whom she sent her photograph in March 1891. A letter from him stated that he could not, or would not, explain why she had returned to Bath, and he was unable to help with the case. There was some discussion regarding Elsie's claim of pregnancy, several witnesses said she did not appear to be so but Superintendent Rutherford remarked that in June she had told him that she was.

Information was also given about a young man, Arthur Burden, a chemist's assistant thought to have frequented Hampton Down. He went missing from Bath in August 1892 – his body was found in the river at Bedminster. This seems to have been disregarded as he came to Bath some months after Elsie disappeared. Three people were then called who had seen Polly on the way to the theatre, but they could not identify the young man with her.

Fig. 117 The George Inn – from the Bathampton Manor
Estate Sale Catalogue, 1921. (Bath Record Office)

The highlight of the inquest was the appearance of Arthur Coombs who wished to give evidence to clear his name now that the court case had finished. He described his relationship with Elsie from spring 1890 to January 1891. He had written her love letters but there was nothing in them to make her think they were engaged and he had never been intimate with her. Whilst seeing her he had walked through Fussells Wood with her, but not in summer 1891 – Phillips and Clare were mistaken. He had seen them there when he was with Polly and Miss Thorne. He denied seeing Elsie after they broke up, except on two occasions when he called at Cheriton House briefly to return some of her things. Mrs Hayman's claim that he was talking to Elsie in Kingsmead Terrace on the Sunday before Bank Holiday was untrue. The brooch found in his room was Elsie's, she had given it to him to get it mended but he dropped it and damaged it. She had said it didn't matter and he had not gone ahead with the repair.

Arthur then gave an account of his movements over the Bank Holiday weekend. On the Saturday he worked in the morning, saw the Volunteers off at the station, then met Clara Thorne at 3.30pm. They walked along the canal towards Bathampton, crossed a bridge and the field to the Warminster Road and had tea at a cottage. They then *went up the lane at right angles to the road*, and returned to Bath in the early evening over Claverton Down.

He arranged to meet her again the following morning, Bank Holiday Monday, the day Elsie was last seen; but it was raining so he stayed in with his brother until midday before calling on her in St James' Square. He came home for tea, and then called on Polly; after going for a short walk they went to the theatre. He denied seeing Elsie that day and only found out she was missing a week later. He had not said much to Polly about it and as for her letter accusing him of being two faced – it referred to Miss Thorne, but she was a cousin of his sister-in-law and his brother had asked him to show her around.

The Coroner then asked him '*Did you murder Elsie Luke or were you concerned in it in any way?*' Arthur replied '*No Sir*'. Clara Thorn corroborated Arthur's evidence and a number of people (his parents, headmaster, employers and the Volunteers) testified to his good character.

Next, William Blick of the Fox and Hounds, Monkton Farleigh, was called and said that when he was at the George Inn late on the morning of Bank Holiday Monday he saw three young men and two girls playing skittles. One might have been Coombs and another was called Dill. One of the girls resembled Elsie, she was wearing ankle boots and a dress similar to the material found on the body. Dill's name was later cleared by William Target of the Volunteers who stated that he had been in camp at Devizes on that day and in any case '*was not given to female society*'. Finally Elizabeth Lane gave evidence – on that Monday she had been on the Downs and had seen a young couple. The woman wore a drab dress that did not fit and a black hat; the man with her was slim and boyish. The Coroner discounted her statement as it was rambling and unsatisfactory.

At last Mr Craddock commenced his summing up in the hot, stuffy room at the George. Elsie had met her death by foul play on or about 3 August 1891. Much evidence had been taken to try to prove that Coombs had a motive – the jury should disregard the court case. They must also disregard Mrs Hayman's evidence, which was unreliable, as she had accused Arthur of going on an outing to Conkwell with Elsie after they split up; in fact it was whilst they were going out together. He then made the following comments on Coombs' statement. If Clare and Phillips saw him walking through Fussells Wood with Elsie it only proved he was '*carrying on*' with her whilst engaged to Polly. Although Mrs Hayman said she saw him talking to Elsie the day before the murder, her evidence was unreliable. Lastly, the police had not disproved his alibi for Bank Holiday.

Strangely the Coroner thought the sighting of the partly clothed man to be a delusion, although Arthur and Frank Clark, who saw him, were likely to be reliable witnesses as their father was headmaster of St Mark's School. In fact if Elsie left Bath at 5pm and the man was seen between 6 and 7pm, this hardly gave time for her to walk up to the Rocks and for him to kill her and conceal the body, although the murderer may have hidden it temporarily and returned later to put it in the cave. It also seems strange that Elsie's history of epilepsy was not considered. Could she have fallen to her death, and her companion, panicking, hid the body? If so, why were the watch and cuff found on the grass at the quarry's edge?

The Coroner regretted that the police had been '*baulked by the lapse of time, much contradictory evidence and suppressing of the truth*'. He severely reprimanded Dill; had he done his duty and handed his findings straight to the police suspicion would have been aroused and had Mrs Kerry read the letters Elsie left behind, extra light might have been thrown on the case. He fined two witnesses for being late and non attendance, reprimanded Mrs Dillon, who for some reason had told Kate Bullock '*not to tell the police all she knew*', and Dill who once again was '*worse for drink*'. He concluded by saying that in his 27 years as Coroner he had never met so many obstacles to an investigation. He could only leave the insoluble problem in the jury's hands.

The jury deliberated for 15 minutes and then reached an open verdict. She had met her death at the hands of some person unknown by being cruelly murdered. Mr Norris, on behalf of the jury, thanked the Coroner and the police for their hard work. Next day the *Bath Chronicle* commented '*After three months no new facts have emerged*'. After seven sessions and taking a mass of evidence, because of Dill's conduct and many obstacles, the Coroner '*could only record a verdict which might have been reached two months ago*'.

On 11 December 1893 the church bell tolled mournfully and Elsie's remains, in a small coffin covered with a black pall, were carried, from the skittle alley at the George, across the road and laid to rest in Bathampton Churchyard.

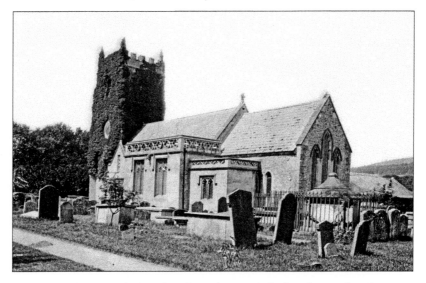

Fig. 118 St Nicholas Church, Bathampton, before the south aisle was built in 1882. (© Bath in Time – Bath Central Library)

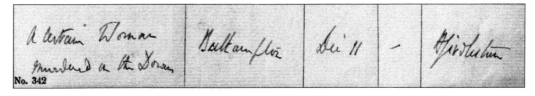

Fig. 119 Entry dated 11 December 1893 in the Bathampton Parish Register of Burials. (Somerset Heritage Centre)

The burial service was conducted by the Rev. H Girdlestone, the only mourners being the policemen Edwards and Brunt and some curious onlookers. None of Elsie's family attended, although both her mother and stepfather were still alive at this date. Apparently the police never traced them but as the tragedy was reported in the press worldwide they probably knew of it. By 1893 they had come up in the world and were proprietors of a coffee house in the East End so perhaps wanted nothing to do with their daughter's notorious demise.

Charles Harper, the Surgeon, obviously moved by Elsie's sad ending, organized a fund to raise £5 for a headstone. A fund was also raised to help Arthur Coombs' father, who had spent his life savings on his son's defence. By 2005 the headstone had degraded badly and was replaced by a replica of more durable stone. This was paid for with part of a legacy left to Bathampton in 1998 by Miss Lucy Barlow, whose family had played an important part in the life of the village.

Arthur Coombs became a local preacher and oral tradition has it that around 1912 he travelled from Bath each Sunday to preach at Bathampton. He always kept his thumb, supposedly scarred from a bite inflicted by Elsie, clenched inside his fist as the Sunday School children would try to see it.[1] Arthur married Polly Sheppard at St Paul's, Bath on 28 November 1895. Eventually they decided to escape the sniggering and innuendo and sailed for Canada, arriving on 8 May 1913. They both died in Victoria, British Columbia; Polly in 1946 and Arthur, aged 78, in 1952; they had no children.

Local people also remembered a cross cut in the turf, which was always kept neatly trimmed, next to the quarry where the murder took place.[2] Many years ago cameras were set up to try to discover who maintained it – one night they were all tripped but the pictures were blurred so the mystery remained. Could it have been the same person who put a notice to Elsie in the *Bath Chronicle* on 11 August 1906, '*Vengeance is mine saith the Lord, I will repay*'?

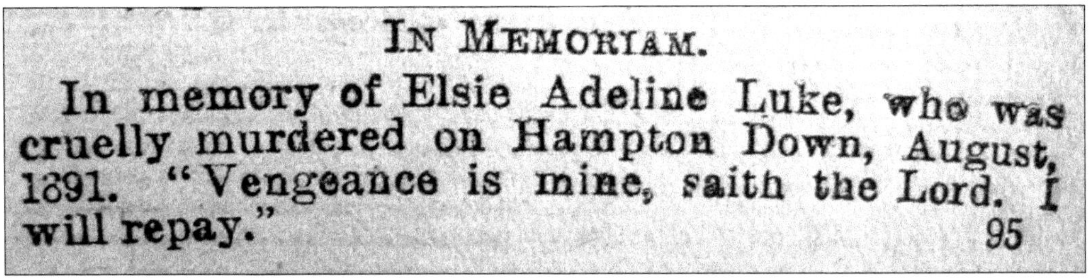

In Memoriam.

In memory of Elsie Adeline Luke, who was cruelly murdered on Hampton Down, August, 1891. "Vengeance is mine, saith the Lord. I will repay."

95

Fig. 120 Memorial Notice in the *Bath Chronicle*, 11 August 1906.
(By permission of the British Newspaper Archive)

Twenty-two years later the *Chronicle* published a letter lamenting the cutting down of trees on either side of the rough path through Fussells Wood to Hampton Down. One was the tree mentioned at Arthur's trial '*on which two amateur athletes had fixed a trapeze*'.[3] Lastly, in 1969, the Bathampton Churchwarden added a note to Elsie Luke's burial record card, '*a long time after, a man in Australia made a death-bed confession to her murder*'. Could this have been Arthur when he died in Canada?

The story of Elsie's murder continues to fascinate and has featured in the local press on numerous occasions since then. Despite all the speculation and rumour it seems that the identity of her killer will never be revealed and the mystery will remain unsolved.

A WARTIME SECRET
The Bathampton Auxiliary Unit Patrol

Forty years later the quarry in which Elsie Luke was found was the scene of further 'secret' activities. Early in 1940, when the threat of German invasion appeared imminent, Churchill ordered a resistance organisation to be set up by GHQ Home Forces. An intelligence officer named Alan Crick organised the Resistance, or Auxiliary, Units in Somerset and Dorset. The Bath City Unit had five patrols, one of which was based at Bathampton; this consisted of a Sergeant and seven men, all of whom had been carefully vetted before being asked to join. They were all men with good local knowledge, and were recruited under conditions of extreme secrecy. Although local to the Bath area, none of them came from Bathampton, and most of them knew little about the other patrol members.

Each patrol was given designated targets and had to set up a secret Operational Base. The Bathampton Patrol, whose Sergeant was an ex-quarryman, found a well hidden cave in the disused limestone quarries on Bathampton Down to use as their hideout. They concealed the narrow entrance with a stone slab covered with earth and stones to simulate a rock fall. The men had to crawl in for six to eight feet then go through a small opening on the right which led down a scree slope to a large cavern. A living area was set up here and some armaments were hidden.

Fig. 121 The Auxiliaries' cave can be seen in the centre.
(G M Huggins, 2013)

Fig. 122 Close up of the cave entrance. (G M Huggins, 2013)

This cave was situated near the Bushy Norwood end of the quarries; the entrance can still be seen (OS ST 778.651) but a rock fall inside means that the hideout cannot now be accessed. After the patrol had completed the task of fitting out the cave they seldom visited it; if they had to do so they carefully covered their tracks by making use of some of the readily available rabbit droppings.

They met on two evenings each week and at weekends for training and had to familiarise themselves with every detail of the local area. The men walked the countryside for miles around until they knew every gap in the hedge, every barn, track and place in which to hide; in the town and villages they explored every corner and alleyway. They went down the Stone Mines at Combe Down and practised keeping watch on the main Warminster Road from the grounds of Claverton Manor. Early on they were sent to the Auxiliary Unit's Headquarters, Coleshill House near Swindon, for army training in the use of weapons. The whereabouts of the HQ was kept secret by driving them on an extremely roundabout route to get there.

The unit was issued with a number of weapons including pistols, fighting knives, rifles and a Thompson submachine gun. They also had an arms/explosives dump on Claverton Down. This was damaged in the air raids of 1942 and had to be moved to Manor Farm at Swainswick, owned by Captain Malcolm Shackell the Area Intelligence Officer. They carried out some training in the use of explosives in the remoter woodlands of the Limpley Stoke Valley; this was difficult because of the need for secrecy.

In the event of invasion they were to receive an emergency signal – the code phrase 'The sun is rising'. They all kept a bag ready packed and had access to a small van. Two members were to drive to the top of Bathwick Hill and from there follow the bridleway to Hampton Down. This ran to a small copse, near the reservoir, where they were to meet up with the rest of the patrol who had been to check on the safety of the Operational Base a short distance away.

Their tasks were to hinder the Germans by sabotaging specific targets:

1. The Railway Junction at Bathampton. (To prepare for this they surveyed the line looking for places where they could place explosive charges).

2. Claverton Manor – should it be occupied by the enemy.

3. The Engine sheds at Green Park Station in Bath.

4. Colerne Airfield. (In autumn 1941 they carried out a successful sabotage exercise against aircraft on the airfield perimeter).

They were not the only unit which had an operational base in the Bathampton area. The Admiralty in Bath had five patrols; their Number Three Patrol had a hideout where the parish boundary, marked by a stream from Hampton Rocks, meets the track from the Warminster Road to Claverton Manor (OS ST 780.652). The Bathampton Patrol (to their great delight) very soon discovered this as it was not far from their cave.

Fortunately the danger of invasion had gone by the middle of 1942 and the Auxiliary Units were stood down in November 1944.

The whole operation was so clandestine that information on the Units comes mainly from the memories of those involved. In 2000 there was a reunion of the Bathampton Patrol and they visited the site of the cave.

One member, Bob Millard, put his memories on the internet, and gave permission for them to be used as a basis for this piece.[1] Official records hardly exist; the names of men involved were included in lists of Home Guard Members in order to conceal their activities. Document WO 199/3390 held by the National Archives lists some names but does not include Bathampton.

Bob Millard gives his fellow patrol members as:
J G Wylde (Sergeant); A Bentley Hunt; W J Denning; J Giles; A C Hannah; G James; J M Jones; P Dahl and A Fieldhouse.

Fig. 123 Bob Millard in 1940, aged 19

Until recently the work of those involved in this secret organisation was quite unknown. We must be extremely grateful to these brave men as there is no doubt of the threat that existed in 1940 and the value of the service given by their Units. Unlike the Home Guard, which was organised by the army, the quite separate Auxiliaries were regarded as civilians and would have been shot on sight by the enemy had invasion occurred. They were, as their motto said, always '*Ready to serve if called*'.

NO LONGER DIVIDED

Fig. 124 Looking eastwards across Bathampton Down towards the old quarries and 11th green.
(M F Clark, 2013)

By the end of the 19th century the division of the Down into two parts no longer applied although they are still often called Hampton Down and Hampton Warren and continue to be shown as such on modern OS maps (see page 1). With the whole of the plateau, the eastern quarry area and northern slopes now coming under the ownership of the Bath Golf Club, the Down is more generally referred to as Bathampton Down.

Due to the nature of their subjects the next sections relating to water sources, the Bathampton Waterworks and the Hampton Down Reservoirs, cannot easily be split between the two halves and mostly refer to the Down as a whole.

They not only give a background to the need for water by the increasing population of Bathampton but trace the most recent major changes to the Down – the building of reservoirs and communication masts to meet the requirements of other areas.

FROM RAINFALL TO RESERVOIRS

Section I
Springs Arising on Bathampton Down

The historic City of Bath is famous not only for its Roman Baths and Georgian Buildings but also for its beautiful setting in a valley surrounded by the southern outcrops of the Cotswold Hills. One noticeable feature of these is their almost level summits, the plateaux of which provide excellent catchment areas for rainwater. From ancient times the springs on the hillsides have provided supplies for Bath and the nearby villages.

Rain falling on these hilltops seeps down through their limestone capping (the Great Oolite) until it reaches an impenetrable layer of Fuller's Earth. Here it emerges a short distance below the plateaux as the 'Upper Springs' which vary in their rate of flow depending on the amount of rainfall. Some water filters down through cracks in the Fuller's Earth until it reaches the Liassic Clays where it emerges near the foot of the hills as the 'Lower Springs' which provide more reliable sources and are less likely to be polluted.

The Upper Springs

Bathampton Down, which at its highest point is almost 670 feet above sea level, has no water sources on its plateau but is similar to neighbouring hills in having a line of 'Upper Springs' rising just below the 500 foot contour. These springs, once so essential to the village and its farmers, were managed by the Bathampton Estate before it was sold in 1921 – pipes were unblocked[1] and stream beds cleared by the estate workers. Subsequently, maintenance of the springs has been minimal, with the exception of a group near the top of the St George's Hill Track. In addition, the hillsides have become overgrown as a result of the decline in their use for farming, making the springs difficult to locate.

Their sites are marked 1 to 8 on the plan on page 132 and detailed as follows:

No. 1: This spring marks the parish boundary between Bathampton and Claverton, emerging in woodland at the eastern end of the Down. Its source is immediately below 'a massive projection of the limestone scarp overlooking the Limpley Stoke Valley'[2] known as Herc's (or Heric's) Promontory – both stream and promontory were mentioned in an Anglo-Saxon Charter of 956 in which King Eadwig granted 5 hides of land at Hampton to his 'faithful liegeman Hehelm'. The charter describes the eastern parish boundary as running 'Up from the Avon on the Mere-broc or boundary brook to the pierced stone; straight up to the southern part of Heric's headland'.[3] The boundary and stream follow a similar course today but the stream now empties into the Canal instead of the river. Herc's Promontory lies on the boundary immediately below a small iron gate on the footpath leading from the south-eastern end of the old Bathampton quarry workings into the corner of Bushy Norwood – a field in Claverton parish now owned by the National Trust.

Fig. 125 Drawing of Herc's Promontory, date and source unknown. Showing part of the boundary wall and gate to Bushy Norwood.

Figs. 126 and 127 Remains of boundary wall below Promontory and trough on boundary stream.
(G M Huggins, 2012)

There was a place in the wood below the Promontory where the stream fell over a rocky outcrop; here the local lads once had great fun 'skinny dipping'. This waterfall was only known to the older boys who did not disclose its whereabouts to their sisters or the younger children. Sadly the land has slipped and it is no longer there, the stream having spread out in places on its journey down through the trees.

No. 2: Further west more springs are found, which supplied water to cattle troughs on the hillside and in the fields below – the remains of this system can still be seen. An overspill from one of the troughs ran down the edge of the bridleway and then followed the side of Down Lane before turning right into the High Street; here it flowed through a channel bridged by stone slabs which gave access to the roadside properties. It then ran down a drain from where it was once piped to an open sewer, a ditch through the fields adjacent to Mill Lane, before emptying into the river. This arrangement probably continued until Bathampton began to be connected to the main sewerage system in 1890. By 1934 the High Street channel had been concreted over.[4] Any overspill is now channelled into main drainage on the Warminster Road.

Fig. 128 High Street from the west with Dog's Head, drainage channel and bridges, c1922. (© Bath in Time – Dafnis Collection)

No. 3: Below the site of the small Roman farmstead and just above the top of the St George's Hill Track are an important group of springs beside Fussells Wood which were the main source of water for Bathampton for many years (see Section II). One still flows down to Bathampton Lane where it formerly filled a horse trough opposite the old Vicarage (now St Nicholas House). Today the stream is diverted into a drain.

Fig. 129 Old horse trough in Bathampton Lane. (M F Clark, 2016)

No. 4:   On the other side of Fussells Wood were another group of springs; one of these, now dried up, ran down through the wood to supply a horse trough beside the Warminster Road, this can still be found buried deep in the grass verge. Another was piped to supply the Warren Farm pond; the site for the farmhouse would have been chosen to take advantage of this nearby source of water.

Fig. 130 St George's Hill Track with old horse trough on left, c1926.
(© Bath in Time – Dafnis Collection)

No. 5:   The spring line continues along the contour, leaving Bathampton parish to run through Bathwick Wood. A small stream rising here marks the western parish boundary as it runs down towards the Warminster Road.

Nos. 6, 7 and 8: This final group of 'Upper Springs', which once supplied Bath and Bathwick, rise in and below the western end of Bathwick Wood and below Sham Castle. Although in the parish of Bathwick they are included here as they are just below the Bathampton boundary and their water originates from the Down's catchment area. In 1769 the Bath Corporation, faced with the rapid expansion of the Georgian City, increased its existing supply by acquiring some of these springs from William Johnstone Pulteney. In return he was granted permission to build Pulteney Bridge to link his new housing development at Bathwick to Bath – on condition that the water was piped over it to feed the City. Some of the springs also supplied the new Pulteney Estate. Bath's water requirements were continually increasing and in 1839 the Corporation acquired more of the springs to supply the growing population. Many of the original spring heads, reservoirs and numbered marker stones can still be seen today.[5]

In 2008 one of these spring boundary markers was found, on its side and covered with undergrowth, immediately in front of Sham Castle on the Bathwick side of the parish boundary. Now it has been re-erected in its original position the lettering on it can clearly be seen; on the south face is the inscription BCW N14, indicating that it was first put in place by Bath City Waterworks in the 18th or 19th century. However it may have had an earlier use as on the east and west sides are letters, which appear to be 'RL' deeply inscribed in a much earlier form of script. A list of lettering used in the 17th century[6] suggests that the 'R' may be an 'A' which would give 'AL' – possibly standing for Anstey's Lodge which was previously on the site of Sham Castle and is discussed in the chapter on 'The Warren'.

Fig. 131 (left) Engraved marker stone. See also Fig 189. (G M Huggins, 2008)

Fig. 132 (above) Letters 'A' and 'L' from *A General Alphabet of Old Law Hands.*

The Sham Castle springs continued in use until they were contaminated in 1928 by a leak from the Golf Club House sewerage system, which was connected to a cess pit at that time. As a result there was an outbreak of typhoid in Bath – 32 people were affected and five died. The supply to Bath and Bathwick was then discontinued and diverted to feed into the Canal; however three properties still took private supplies from springs in the area. One of these was the Trossachs [now Columbus House] in Bathampton, a Victorian mansion set high above the Warminster Road at the far western side of the parish. In 1932 the Ministry of Health advised that a reliable supply should be connected but the owner, Mr Hutchings, was happy to continue using the spring water at his own risk as it was regularly tested.[7] In 1966 the property was sold to a Mr Moore who planned to turn it into a Motel and the Corporation agreed to try to give it a mains supply. The Motel was never established and a main to the Trossachs was not completed until 1973 when a development of luxury homes was built in its grounds.

The Lower Springs

The 'Lower Springs' arise at the foot of the hillside approximately on the 150 foot contour and are numbered 9 to 13 on the map -

No. 9: This spring emerges on the far eastern side of the parish; it still provides a private supply to what was Holcombe Farm [now Holcombe Villa].

No. 10: In Bathampton High Street is the well known Dog's Head Trough – an attractive feature in the village. It is fed by a '*never failing spring*' which for centuries was the main water supply for nearby properties. This rises a little further up the hillside and probably accounts for the establishment of a Roman Villa, remains of which were discovered in the 19th century in the area of today's playing field and allotments. It is piped down towards the road then passes through a garden wall where it pours from a curious, stone, dog's head into a large stone trough at the roadside.

Fig. 133 Dog's Head trough.
(M F Clark, 2015)

No. 11: On leaving the village centre and travelling towards Bath, Court Leet, once three late seventeenth century cottages, is on the left. Outside its gates are a mounting block and a shallow, double water trough alongside the garden wall, behind which is another trough. Both were once fed by a nearby spring but this is no longer the case, as when an adjacent property was built the underground source of the spring was disturbed and the water piped away.

Figs. 134 and 135 Troughs at Court Leet. (M F Clark, 2016)

No. 12: A little further along on the right, is the Old Rectory – part of which probably dates from the late 16th Century. There has been a property here since 1317, when the benefice of Bathampton was ordained as part of the monastery of St Peter and St Paul, Bath and a *'competent dwelling house'* was built for the priest.

Fig. 136 The Old Rectory from Bathampton Lane. (R Russell, 2007)

Near the Old Rectory and at the adjacent Glebe Cottage a group of springs emerge; one of these, also a *'never failing spring'*, is piped into a tank under the Rectory driveway. In 1939 the Bath Waterworks Engineer estimated the flow at 14,000 gallons per day,[8] it is certainly substantial as at one time it augmented the village supply in periods of drought (see Section II). It still provides enough water for an ornamental lake behind the house [formerly the monks' fishpond] the outfall of which drains into the Canal. One of the Glebe Cottage springs was piped through the Old Rectory's front garden, and was still supplying several properties to the east in 1921.[9] Parts of the first two [now called Kennet Court and Bathampton House] were used as the Bathampton Laundry. This enterprise, established by the Allens, was run by the Stacey family from 1874 to 1912. The pipe from Glebe Cottage also supplied the original Bathampton House [a Georgian Mansion that once stood on the site of Kennet Park] and the following property, Manor Farm [now 13 – 15 Harbutts].

Nos. 13 to 16: The lower spring line gives rise to four more springs as it continues just above the Canal to the western parish boundary. Further springs emerge after it passes into Bathwick. Immediately on the Bathwick side of the boundary, near the Grosvenor Bridge, once stood the Folly Inn and the adjacent Grosvenor Brewery. These made good use of the spring water before they were destroyed by enemy bombing in World War II.

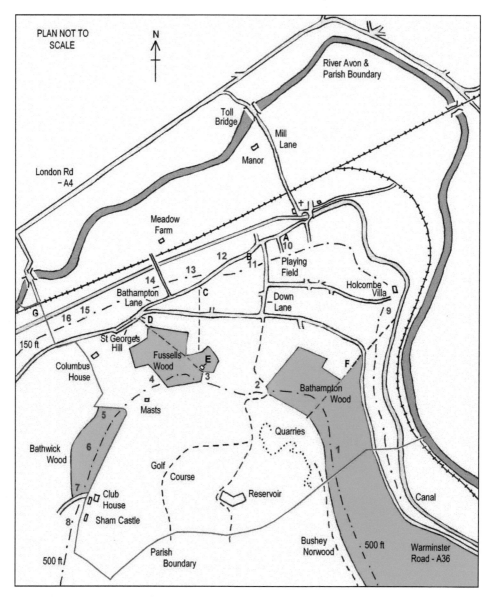

Fig. 137 Plan of Spring Lines in Bathampton Parish (M F Clark, 2016)

Nos. 1 – 8 Upper Springs
Nos. 9 – 16 Lower Springs
A – Dog's Head Trough
B – Court Leet Troughs

C – Bathampton Lane Trough
D – Warminster Road Trough
E – Site of Bathampton Tank
F – Tramway

G – Site of Folly Inn

FROM RAINFALL TO RESERVOIRS

Section II
Bathampton Waterworks and earlier sources

The location of early settlements depended largely on the availability of a plentiful supply of water. Bathampton was ideally sited on the lower spring line at the foot of the Downs with the Dog's Head spring occupying a central position in the main street and the Old Rectory springs on the outskirts of the village. This section will describe how supplies in Bathampton were drawn from these local springs until the Allen family set up their Waterworks in the late 19th Century and why this undertaking ran into difficulties as the village expanded.

Early Water Sources

The first documentary evidence for the construction of a private water supply in Bathampton dates from 1347-48 when the Lord of the Manor, James Husee, was granted permission by Ralph de Salopia, Bishop of Bath and Wells, to run a conduit to his house in the parish '*from Choldewelle on Hampton Hill*'.[10] Unfortunately no other details are given of the location of the spring or the house. Five hundred years later another Lord of the Manor also had his own water supply – from a different spring and almost certainly to a different house. A proposal was put forward under the Bath Waterworks Act of 1846[11] to obtain water for the City from the Old Rectory springs – this protected the '*right accustomed*' of the Lord of the Manor, George Edward Allen, to take water from the springs. To supply his premises this was piped 300 yards to a trough which stood on his land '*on the south side or near to the embankment of the GWR*'. In the cellar of Bathampton Manor there is still a large slate water tank once fed by a pipe, presumably to store water running from the trough to the house.[12]

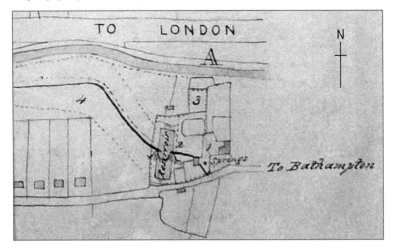

Fig. 138 Plan of Old Rectory from proposed 1846 scheme.
Landowners: Nos. 1-3 Robert Fisher; 4 G E Allen. (Bath Record Office)

Fortunately for Bathampton the Corporation's scheme was never implemented as the Old Rectory Springs were later to provide an essential supply for the village; instead two reservoirs were built at Batheaston in 1848 to supply Bath. Meanwhile, the majority of those living in Bathampton High Street were using the copious supply gushing from the Dog's Head for most of their requirements (supplemented by two pumps in Chapel Row).

In 1883 the Medical Officer of Health, Dr Charles Harper, reported on 20 villages in the Bath Area.[13] He stated that there was little overcrowding in these communities but the sanitary state of some was far from satisfactory owing to filth and structural defects. The poor, he said, needed '*training in cleanliness*' and their health was dependant on their water supply. It appears that the population of Bathampton did not have too many of these problems as his table of mortality shows only two deaths in the village that year and they '*did not properly belong to the parish*'; in addition there were none caused by whooping cough, measles, typhoid or scarlet fever. The only cause for concern was the smell from the Avon – sewage tanks at Bathford emptied straight into it, floating sewage washed up on the river banks and the smell was complained of '*as far as Bathampton Bridge*'. Bathampton's sewage also drained into the river as connection to the main drains was not begun until the 1890s.

Fig. 139 Notice above Dog's Head Trough. (G M Huggins, 2015)

At about the same time mains water was laid on in the village and by 1943 only six properties in the High Street still took their supply from the Dog's Head – although others used it for washing purposes as they thought the spring water was softer. In that year a sample was found to be contaminated, a stand pipe was erected near the trough and a sign '*water unfit to drink*' fixed to the wall behind it.[14] The pipe is no longer there but the sign can still be seen.

The following memories[15] are from some Bathampton residents who lived in the village before mains water was laid on :

Maurice Lewis –
'*Water was carried to the allotments using a wooden yoke with two buckets borne on a strong man's shoulders*'.

Frances Fritsche (*née* Fennell) –
'*My Grandparents, Wm and Charlotte Netherwood, lived in a cottage in the grounds of Harbutts* [factory]. *Water for everything was taken from the Dog's Head.*' Later, piped water was laid on.

Phyllis Ford (*née* Noad) –
'*When I lived at 7 Chapel Row as a child we were lucky to have a water pump right outside our door serving several households which provided ice-cold water all year round. In summer the bus drivers were grateful for a cool refreshing drink. It was the purest water you could get and residents missed it when a mains supply was provided. A second pump was in Mrs Hunt's garden at Myrtle Cottage; this was sealed off and paved over when the cottages were converted into flats and the gardens made into a parking space*'.

There were also three properties in the High Street which had their own supplies – Yew Tree Cottage and Mount Pleasant had wells behind them; the third, Bathampton Lodge (a sixteenth century house with later additions) had a hot and cold bath house in its garden, possibly once run as a commercial enterprise. Built in about 1800 this was originally a cold plunge bath, fed from a pump, but later a furnace house was constructed at the side of the building so that either hot or cold baths could be taken.[16] The bath house was tastefully restored in 2005 and now makes an attractive garden feature.

Fig. 140 Restored Bath House from the west.
(R Russell, 2008)

Until just after World War II water supplies in England were provided on a local level by town corporations or small, private waterworks companies. Prior to the sale of the Bathampton Estate in 1921, the Lord of the Manor held the rights to all water from springs in the parish; for example he made an agreement with the GWR to supply Bathampton Station from the overflow of the Old Rectory pond. There is also evidence that he provided water to some of the grander houses in the parish, piped direct from springs on Hampton Down. The deeds for Hessle House (one of four large villas built in Bathampton Lane in the early 19th century) state that if John Pullin, the purchaser, '*should at any time think proper to supply the premises with a good and sufficient quantity of water*' he must obtain this from George Edward Allen, the vendor, who would supply him at the usual prices charged by the Bath Corporation *'in respect of houses in the City'*.[17]

Fig. 141 Old Rectory Fish Pond. (R Russell, 2008)

In 1882 residents of six properties *'near the City boundary on Hampton road'* asked Major Ralph Shuttleworth Allen (George Edward's successor and nephew) to *'undertake a water scheme for Bathampton'* but although he *'received the suggestion favourably'* nothing was done.[18] The residents, including William J Wilcox of Hampton Hall, then applied to the Bath Corporation for a supply and in 1886 the City's Cold Water Committee agreed to extend the main on the Hampton Road at a cost of £90.[19] Major Allen, obviously upset by this, stated that he could supply all the houses in the district at a much cheaper rate than the Corporation from a *'source on a level nearly equal to that of Sham Castle, giving a fall of 300 feet and yielding between 50,000 and 60,000 gallons per day'*.[20] This refers to the springs near the top of the St George's Hill Track. The Corporation delayed proceeding but eventually the six properties were connected to the Bath mains.

The Bathampton Waterworks

Major Allen died on the 2 February 1887 and was succeeded by his son Col. Ralph Edward Allen who established the Bathampton Waterworks to give the expanding village a proper supply. This undertaking probably opened in about 1890 as the ordnance survey map for 1888[21] shows that the tank (or reservoir) for the scheme was not yet built, but by August 1891[22] a supply from the Waterworks was laid on to the first Bathampton School during the summer holiday – its well water having been condemned by the School Inspector. From 1859 this school stood in a small paddock, south of the church, now incorporated into the churchyard. It was replaced by the present school which was erected nearby in 1896. During the following year the new building was supplied with drinking water by the Waterworks, however the toilets at the bottom of the school yard were flushed with water pumped from a well – as this often ran dry buckets of water had to be brought from the Canal until a metered supply from the Waterworks was installed in 1905. The outside toilets were finally brought up to standard in 1968 with washbasins and heating and were demolished in 1989 when the school was extended. During the building work the old well was discovered at the bottom of the toilet block.[23]

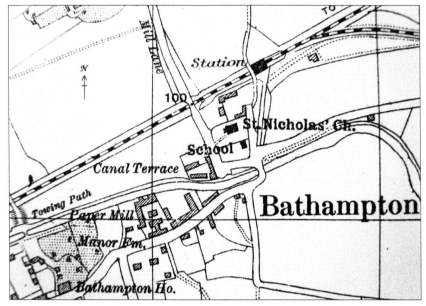

Fig. 142 Extract from R F Houlston's undated Plan of Bath showing the old school south of the church. (Bath Record Office)

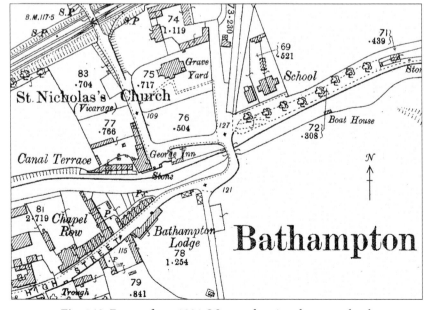

Fig. 143 Extract from 1904 OS map showing the new school, school house and toilet block, east of the church. (Bath Record Office)

The tank for the Waterworks which supplied the school and the village was sited in woodland on the north-east side of the St George's Hill Track and the stored water gravity fed through a pipeline to Bathampton about half a mile below. The tank was supplied from the group of springs just above it, near the top of the track, where the occupants of the Roman farmstead once collected their water. As the springs were on the 'Upper Level' there was a serious problem when their rate of flow decreased in times of drought and the level in the tank became low; to combat this extra water was pumped up from the reliable 'Lower Level' Old Rectory springs. The pump was housed in a shed in the garden of Old Cottage, which stands almost opposite the Old Rectory, and was operated and maintained by three successive generations of the White family, who were also responsible for keeping the tank and pipelines in good order. They were employed by the Bathampton Estate and lived in the cottage, enabling them to operate the pump at night when necessary. Thomas James White is the first recorded as 'Waterman' being listed as such in the street directories from 1896; he had occupied Old Cottage for some time as he was living there, working as an Agricultural Labourer, when the 1881 census was taken. After his death in 1900 his son William worked as the Waterman until he died in 1931 – in turn he was succeeded by his son Arthur James, known locally as 'Art'.

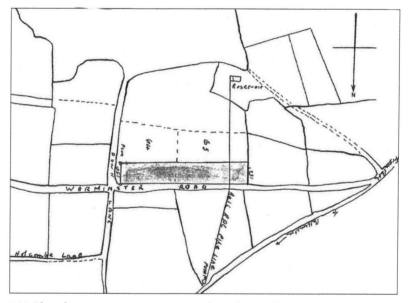

Fig. 144 Plan showing pumping station and pipeline to the reservoir, 1926. (M Borea)

Bathampton Waterworks is purchased by the Rural District Council

By 1914 there were still only a few houses in Bathampton receiving water from the Bath Corporation, the majority obtained it *'from Colonel Allen's private Water Works'.*[24] This situation continued until 1921 when the Bathampton Estate was sold by auction on 6 April. The greater part of the estate was disposed of privately prior to this – including Lot 16, the Waterworks and Old Cottage, which was purchased by the Rural District Council [RDC] for £1,500. After William White died in 1931 his son Arthur continued to tenant the cottage; he was employed by the Council to continue his duties as part time Waterman and, additionally, to work as the village Roadman. His familiar figure could often be seen, complete with polished brown leather gaiters and trilby hat, working with brush, shovel and wheelbarrow to keep the roads in order. He retired as Roadman on 8 August 1955 but stayed on as part-time Waterman until 30 September 1958, when Bath Corporation took over the Waterworks. He continued to live at the Old Cottage until he died, aged 81, in 1969; his wife Mabel was allowed to remain as tenant until her death in 1977. The Old Cottage, which had been her home for 45 years, was then sold.[25]

When the RDC purchased the Bathampton Waterworks in 1921 the sale included not only the cottage but the adjoining pumping station which consisted of a shed (with galvanised iron roof and cement floor) containing a recently installed Glenfield Pump with Kingston Gas Engine.[26]

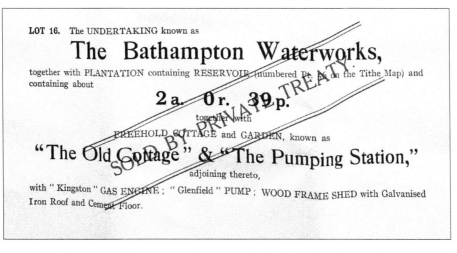

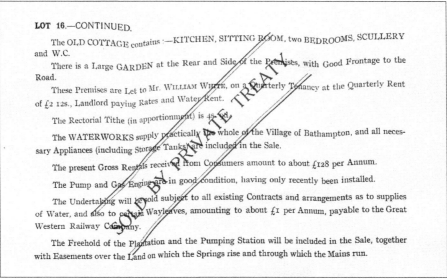

Figs. 145 and 146 Details of the Bathampton Waterworks from Sale catalogue of the Bathampton Manor Estate, 1921. (Bath Record Office)

They also acquired the reservoir in a 2 acre coppice of woodland and 'all springs, water-courses, mains, pipes, tanks, catchpits and other apparatus' used by the Waterworks. Transferred to the Council was a right of way for all purposes along the track to the reservoir from the Warminster Road, easements over the land on which the springs rose and agreements with the GWR dated 1890 and 1892 regarding pipes crossing their bridges in the parish. Lastly, they had to honour an agreement with George D Hunt, the owner of the Old Rectory, to limit the amount of water taken from his spring, so that enough was left to prevent his lake from becoming stagnant.

The sale of the Manorial Estate resulted in a sustained increase in property building at Bathampton, beginning in the early 1920s with ribbon development along the Warminster Road. In 1926, numbers 1 – 15 were built near the Trossachs and Bath Corporation agreed to supply them by extending the main going to the six properties previously mentioned. The remainder of the village, however, was still supplied by the RDC which had provided water to 70 houses when it bought the Bathampton Waterworks in 1921. By 1926 this number had increased to 130.[27]

The following years saw the building of yet more houses along the Warminster Road, in Down Lane and the new developments of St George's Hill and Devonshire Road – all increasing the demand for water. Bath was also facing problems owing to the expansion of the City and had invested in the '1926 Scheme' set up to supply its south side. This involved building a new reservoir on the top of Hampton Down which obtained its water from an existing reservoir, Monkswood, on the opposite side of the Avon Valley (see Section III).

As a result of the increasing population water shortages in Bathampton were becoming more and more acute – especially during hot, dry summers such as that of 1929 which saw a spell of 201 days without rain, the longest for 100 years. During another drought in 1934 residents were complaining that 'water is only a dribble from 9am and will not fill household tanks so toilets will not flush'. In the last nine years 200 new houses had been built but the size of the tank remained the same at 24,000 gallons – it had not been cleaned for 30 years and was cracked so that water was running to waste. The RDC Surveyor, however, stated that 'there was plenty of water to meet demand. The pump [at Old Cottage] was going all day and during the night'.[28]

This was only the beginning of serious problems, particularly for the residents living in the upper part of the village on the Warminster Road, and over the years there were many similar complaints. It was clear that something had to be done. The RDC made the first of many approaches to the Corporation in 1933, asking them to augment the Bathampton supply,[29] they refused to provide partial relief but would consider taking over the whole undertaking. At a meeting in 1936 Councillor Ernest Tucker of Bathampton asked for Bath to be approached again with a view to purchasing the supply, as there were plans for 400 more houses with shops during the next ten years. Although a new tank had been constructed it only held enough for three days – when leaks occurred in the village it soon ran dry. The RDC surveyor once again disagreed saying that 'leaks were soon repaired' and the motion was not seconded.[30]

As the Bath take-over seemed to be going nowhere other options were suggested. One of these was to tap a spring above the Dry Arch and an agreement to purchase it for £100 was made with the landowner, the Bath Golf Club. This scheme did not materialise – it was turned down by the Ministry of Health as it would not give a sufficient supply at all times and the RDC was told to '*look to Bath for water*'.

In 1938, another dry year, the RDC produced a report on Bathampton Waterworks[31] as part of more negotiations with Bath to provide a temporary supply to alleviate the water shortage in the village. This showed that the new tank was considerably larger than the old with a capacity of 33,640 gallons and that there were a total of 3,360 yards of mains supplying 204 houses. The extra supply from the Old Rectory was used during the summer months when water was moved up to the tank at a rate of 1,100 gallons per hour by a new pump, installed in 1930. There was an outstanding loan of almost £1,000 for the new tank and the Waterman's wages plus other expenses totalled £214.

Once again the Corporation agreed to furnish the extra water but only if the RDC agreed to their acquisition of the Waterworks and once again the RDC refused to comply. Meanwhile those living in Bathampton had their water cut off at times and had to '*choose between washing and making tea*' – visitors could only have half a cup.[32] Water used for cooking was '*carefully strained*' and used for other purposes and the villagers worried that there might be an epidemic. In September 1938 a petition signed by 41 residents was sent to the RDC calling upon them '*to do all in their power to put an end to the difficulties and dangers now existing by securing co-operation with the Bath Corporation... the health of communities is of far greater concern than the difficulties of providing a sufficient water supply*'.[33]

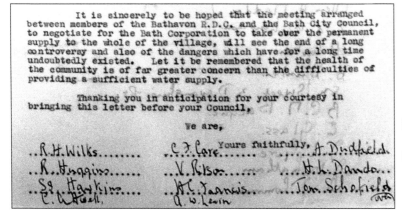

Fig. 147 Extract from petition. (Bath Record Office)

Their pleas fell on deaf ears and the two authorities continued with their impasse. The following year it was found that the RDC had been taking far more than their entitlement of half of the yield from the Old Rectory Springs. Mr Hunt '*could have complained and claimed damages many times when his pond became stagnant but refrained owing to the need of the village for water*'.[34]

During the spring and summer of 1939 yet another attempt was made at a Bath takeover and the Corporation's Engineer made a detailed report on the condition of the Bathampton

Waterworks[35] *'which leaves much to be desired but can be put into a satisfactory condition to give an adequate supply'*. The springs were yielding enough for eight months of the year and the water was suitable and safe for drinking and domestic use. Sterilization equipment would be put in, spring heads reconstructed and protected, the steel tank painted and its corrugated roof repaired. In addition 180 yards of main would be connected to the City's mains to give an extra supply in times of need and the Old Rectory springs would be abandoned as they were unsatisfactory for public use. Unfortunately there was a sticking point, the outstanding loan, now £904, taken out by the Bathampton Waterworks some years before to put in a new tank, which Bath did not want to pay off. In addition some members of the RDC felt the Corporation was trying to extend its boundary and that *'this was their chance to bring Bathampton into the Borough'*. Despite their water problems this opinion was shared by many residents who wished the village to retain its independent status. The arguments continued.

The outbreak of war on 3 September added further to Bathampton's problems. The population of the village increased when evacuees were sent from the East End of London and Admiralty workers were billeted in the village after their department was moved from London to Bath for safety. Despite the extra, heavy demand on the village supply Bath would neither agree to take over the outstanding loan, nor furnish a bulk supply.

Later in 1939 there was an improvement in the Bathampton supply after a serious leak in the rising main to the tank was repaired and there are no further reports of problems for several years – undoubtedly there were more pressing concerns during the earlier years of the war. In January 1944, however, Joseph Woodward, Deputy Senior Captain of the Bathampton Fire Guard, wrote to the Bath Chronicle as he was concerned about a lack of water for fire fighting.

Fig. 148 Members of the Bathampton Auxiliary Fire Service, 1946.
(© Bath Industrial Heritage Trust Ltd)

142

There had been '*a most unwise and reprehensible neglect*' regarding a sufficient supply in the event of another blitz. The Canal was too far from elevated housing in the village to be used in the case of an emergency. The RDC replied that the Regional Office would not agree to the siting of 13,000 gallon tanks in the village and there was ample water in the mains supply for the Fire Guards' limited resources. Ludicrously they suggested that '*if all householders saw to it that a bucket or two of water is kept available for fire fighting the Fire Guards should be able to do what is expected of them*'.[36] Fortunately there was no recurrence of the Bath Blitz of 25-27 April 1942 so their suggestion was not put to the test.

In June 1944, Walter Hughes, fruit and vegetable grower of the Dry Arch Nurseries, also complained to the RDC about the '*disgraceful state of the water supply*' – he had to carry every drop of domestic water from a well in his grounds and several of his neighbours living on the Warminster Road also had difficulties. An extension of the main was considered by the RDC but by September they decided it was futile to put in a temporary pipe as there was to be a big development in that area which would need a full sized main. This left the unfortunate occupier of Woodside, opposite the Nursery, carrying water in buckets from his neighbour as his well had dried up.[37]

During the spring of the following year, when the war was drawing to a close, the RDC drew up plans for a building programme to cope with the expected post war demand for housing and a development of 44 council houses was allocated to Bathampton. A private developer also had plans for a very large housing scheme, the size of a new village, to be built on the eastern side of the parish but this never came to fruition. To supply the new council estate extra water would have to be found and, as there was still no agreement with the Corporation, the RDC began to look for a new source in Bathampton. They engaged J Mullins & Son of Manvers Street, Bath, to drill a test well in a field near to Meadow Farm Canal Bridge; although a good supply was found it was never developed.[38] This may have been because negotiations with Bath took a turn for the better in 1946 when the Bath Waterworks Engineer produced the most detailed report yet on the Bathampton undertaking. It is similar to that of 1939 but with additions – the population of Bathampton was now about 1,100 requiring 15,000 gallons of water per day; 283 properties were supplied; six springs on Hampton Down filled the tank and the supply from the Old Rectory had been chlorinated since 1943. To provide water for the new housing development he suggested that a connection could be made to the Batheaston distribution main via Mill Lane. His estimate of the cost for modernising the Bathampton Waterworks was five to six thousand pounds.[39]

Negotiations with the Corporation were still looking promising in January 1947, by which time the RDC contractors were constructing mains, sewers and roads on the 6 acre site off Holcombe Lane where the new council houses were to be built. Unsurprisingly, by March the deal had fallen through – this time because the Corporation wanted the Old Cottage to be included as part of the package. The RDC, however, would not agree as it was let to their employee, Mr White, and in addition some council members felt that it was '*regarded as a treasure by everybody in the village*'.[40]

Fig. 149 'Old Cottage' with Mr White's barrow and shovel, c1925.
(© Bath in Time – Dafnis Collection)

The Fire Guards' concerns turned out to be well founded when, in May 1948, a fire broke out at 10, 12 and 13 Down Lane and *'three garages were destroyed'*.[41] The Bath Fire Brigade had great difficulty in putting out the flames owing to the insufficient force of water – the pressure in the lane was very low as it only had a two inch main. Local residents were understandably alarmed owing to the proximity of the Warminster Road Petrol Station [Holbrow's Garage]. Shortly afterwards they made representations to the RDC which agreed to put in a new main but the Somerset County Council vetoed the scheme because *'a larger main is of no use as the tank capacity is too small'*. It was unfortunate that nothing was done as on 20 May 1950, the Village Hall in Holcombe Lane was totally destroyed by an arsonist. The lack of water contributed largely to the disaster despite villagers helping the firemen to put out the blaze by running a hose to the Canal 600 yards away. This tragedy for the village prompted the Parish Council to demand that the RDC take immediate action to improve the Bathampton supply.[42] As a result the RDC approached Bath once again but by this time the Corporation had become involved in the Bristol, Bath and Mendip Supply Scheme to obtain water from a new reservoir at Chew Valley; they were willing to proceed but until this was completed they did not have enough resources to do so. However they were able to give some help in 1955 when Bathampton needed more water to supply a new development of about 28 houses and four shops to be erected on the south side of Holcombe Lane by local builder Victor Toogood.

Bath agreed to extend its main to 20 more houses along the south side of the Warminster Road immediately east of St George's Hill – this would free up enough Bathampton Water to supply the new properties. The work, completed in June 1955, formed the first stage of the City's plan to supply the whole village and on 1 October 1958, after more than 20 years of bureaucratic indecision, the acquisition of the Bathampton Waterworks by Bath Corporation was finally accomplished.[43]

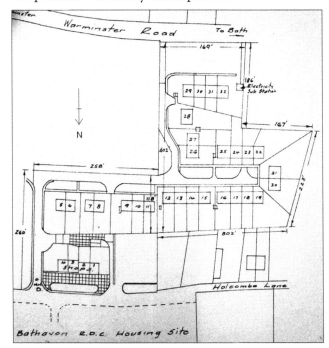

Fig. 150 Plan of the Manor Development (Holcombe Close), 1951. (Bath Record Office)

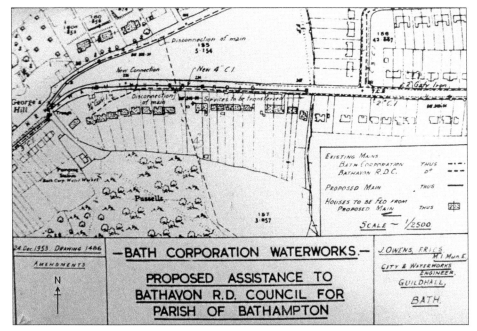

Fig. 151 Plan of the 20 houses (as shaded) to be supplied by Bath, 1958. (Bath Record Office)

Soon after the take-over, during the very dry summer of 1959, the Bath Waterworks Engineer faced inevitable problems with the inadequate Bathampton supply – as a result of this and owing to the danger of pollution in the tank he revised his scheme to increase the amount of water available for the village.[44] First the tank was cleaned, painted and fitted with a new roof, making it ready to be filled with treated water supplied by the Corporation. Conveniently, it was possible for them to construct a branch pipeline to the tank from a nearby main on the south-east – this runs from Monkswood up through Fussells Wood to the Corporation's reservoir on the Down [see Part III]. The tank was then able to provide a safe, clean supply for Bathampton. A further improvement was made by the replacement of a leaking main in the Warminster Road.

The Engineer also realised that for years the lower part of the village had suffered from too much water pressure while those living in the upper part were often trying to manage with too little. To solve this problem his new scheme proposed that the lower houses would be supplied from the Warminster Road main and the higher from the refurbished tank in the woods. It was hoped that at last this would give '*a complete answer to water problems in Bathampton Village*'.

Water from the Old Rectory Springs was not needed after the new inlet main to the tank was constructed. The pump at Old Cottage became redundant and its familiar 'thud, thud' was no longer heard in Bathampton Lane. The Corporation retained its rights to the Springs until 1966, when water started to run down the Old Rectory drive and repairs had to be made. This expense prompted Bath to relinquish its rights as it had no further use for the Springs.

The tank was still in use in 1970 when it was again cleaned and painted, the compound cleared and part of the inlet main re-laid. Four years later Wessex Water took over supplies in the Bath Area and in 2008 they demolished the old tank, which had become redundant. After over 100 years the last vestiges of the local Waterworks set up by the Allen family had disappeared.

Fig. 152 Name plate on the gate of the Bathampton tank. (G M Huggins, 2009)

Fig. 153 Site of the Bathampton tank after demolition. (G M Huggins, 2009)

Today Wessex Water no longer captures the water from the springs which supplied the old tank; instead it is drained into the River Avon. Bathampton village now receives its water from the Hollies Lane Reservoir, Batheaston, which feeds much of the north side of Bath. This reservoir is filled by springs at Monkswood, Batheaston and Oakford along with a supply from North Wiltshire.

FROM RAINFALL TO RESERVOIRS

Section III
Reservoirs on the Summit

What appears to be one large reservoir on the top of Hampton Down is actually four conjoined on a single site. Originally there was one circular reservoir, constructed in the late 1920s, but over the years three more have been added and the whole complex surrounded by an earthen bank. It would be logical to assume that these reservoirs were built to take advantage of water available from springs nearby but this is not the case as they are all filled with water pumped up from sources several miles away. Their high position on the summit of the Down ensures that their contents can be gravity fed easily to other areas, principally the south side of Bath. Surprisingly, it seems that they have never supplied the parish of Bathampton; neither did another much smaller reservoir built on the Warren in 1890 and demolished in 1958.

The Combe Down Waterworks Reservoir

A small private company was set up in 1881 to supply Combe Down with water pumped up from springs at Tucking Mill, near Midford, to an elevated tank on the Bradford Road. Over the years this undertaking had several changes of name and ownership but was generally referred to as the Combe Down Waterworks Company. In 1888 plans were made to expand by supplying houses in Bathwick and Widcombe and, as part of this scheme, a new reservoir was needed. A suitable site was found on the Warren and leased for 99 years from Col. Ralph Edward Allen on 22 November 1890.[45] The Combe Down Waterworks Company Reservoir *'of not less capacity than 50,000 gallons'* was then constructed in the south-eastern corner of the Golf Course.

The reservoir measured 61 feet by 20 feet 6 inches and was built of stone. At first it was fed with water via the Combe Down distribution main but in 1906 this arrangement was replaced by a six inch main laid to Hampton Down from springs at Tucking Mill.

In 1907 a pipe to take water to the Golf Club House from the reservoir was installed[46] and in the same year the Waterworks Company signed an agreement with Bath Corporation to supply high level areas on the south side of the City between Bathwick Hill and Odd Down.[47] After this agreement lapsed in 1931 a large new reservoir built on Hampton Down by the Bath Corporation took over the supply to these areas.[48] The small Combe Down Waterworks Reservoir remained in use supplying other districts including Combe Down, Monkton Combe, Limpley Stoke and Winsley.

It appears that it also continued to supply the Golf Club as in early 1949 they complained that they had had no water since before Christmas – the Water Company *'suggested that there must be a leak in the pipe as the reservoir was full. It turned out, after Mr Mannings had checked and found the pipe to be unbroken, that the reservoir was empty. The Fire Brigade sent 300 gallons to help'.*[49]

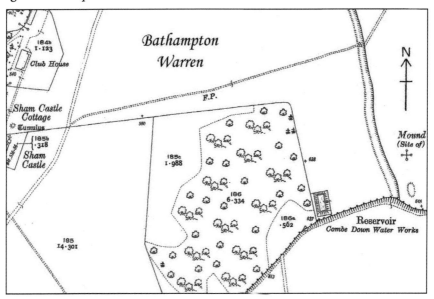

Fig. 154 Extract from OS Map, 1932, Sheet XIV 2,
showing site of Combe Down Reservoir. (Bath Record Office)

After a number of unsuccessful attempts the Bath Corporation finally purchased the Combe Down Waterworks Company for £25,000 in December 1954, ending over 70 years of a successful private venture. New arrangements were then made for the Golf Club and early in 1955 Mr Mannings reported to the Committee – *'The Clubhouse is supplied by a half inch main until recently connected to the Combe Down Water Works Reservoir, which has often been at a low level. However, Bath Water Works acquired the Water Works six months ago, have dispensed with the reservoir and the Golf Club is now on their mains'.* At last the problems with their water supply had been resolved.

By March 1955 the reservoir had become redundant and the new owners enquired whether the Bath Golf Club, which had become the lessor when it bought Hampton Down and the Warren from the Allen family in 1921, would surrender the lease which still had over 30 years to run. After some hard bargaining the Club agreed to do so for a payment of £100, provided the Bath Corporation dismantled the surrounding fence, collapsed the walls inwards, levelled the land, made good any damage, removed the reservoir's corrugated iron roof and timbers and *'left them stacked for Golf Club use'.* These terms were agreed and the surrender of the land took place on 29 September 1958; the reservoir was to be demolished by Christmas Day but it is likely that the City Waterworks Engineer had the work carried out well before that as he was anxious about the danger to trespassing school children.

All that can be seen today is a rough area of ground in the corner behind the present ninth tee and a small iron gate in the parish boundary wall between the University Campus and the Golf Course, which was formerly the entrance to the reservoir.

148

Fig. 155 Original Gate to the Combe Down Reservoir, with securing chain.
(M F Clark, 2015)

The 1926 Scheme

By the first half of the 1920s the small Combe Down Waterworks Reservoir was struggling to supply enough water to the south side of Bath and it became necessary for the Bath Waterworks Committee to address this problem. In August 1926 they contracted John Mullins and Son, Waterfinders and Waterworks Engineers of Railway Place, to search for new sources of supply for the high areas from Bathwick to Odd Down. Mullins found a number of springs but all proved inadequate and he reported that the Corporation would be better '*to obtain a supply from its present system at Monkswood*'.[50]

The large Monkswood Reservoir, capacity 51 million gallons, was opened in 1897 to supply Bath.[51] It is situated high in the hills to the north of the City at the head of St Catherine's Valley and is supplied from high level springs rising in the parish of Cold Ashton to the north and on the slopes of Charmy Down to the south. Water from it is gravity fed down a main to Batheaston where it joins the London Road (A4) main and continues into the City.

Mullins suggested that a nine inch branch pipeline should be taken from the 18 inch London Road main at Lambridge. It would run south, cross the River Avon at the Grosvenor Bridge, pass under the Great Western Railway (GWR) and the Canal then continue uphill through the Hampton House Paddock to the Warminster Road (A36). A pumping station would then have to be constructed south of the road to pump the water on uphill to the top of Hampton Down, where it would fill a new reservoir built to supply the south side of the City.

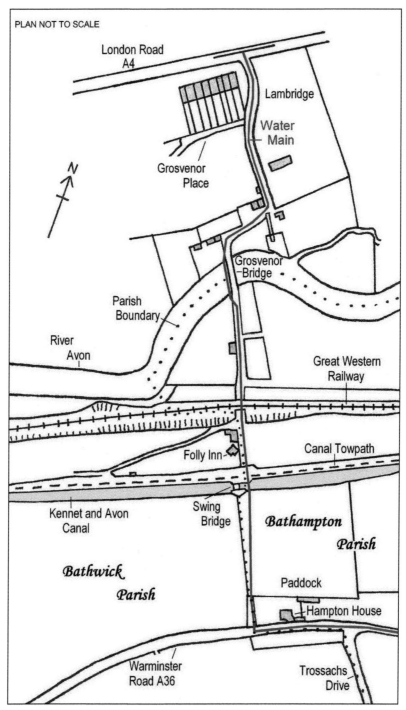

Fig. 156 Plan of the 1926 main running from the A4 to the A36 based on
plans held by Bath Record Office. (M F Clark, 2016)

In September 1926 the Waterworks Committee agreed to proceed with this scheme
and build a circular 400,000 gallon reservoir on the highest point of Hampton Down

(OS ST 774.649). As this would be on the golf course negotiations began to purchase 100 square feet of land from the Club and arrange easements for the main with all the landowners involved.

The 1926 scheme, with an estimated cost of about £30,000, proceeded slowly with a great deal of planning, preparation and hard work. Mullins had suggested that the main should cross the river via the footbridge at Grosvenor, however as this was a suspension bridge, built in 1850 by T Shew, it would need replacing with a more substantial concrete structure designed to carry the pipeline on its western side. To avoid this expense various other schemes were suggested, including divers laying the pipe across the river bed at Bathampton Bridge, but in the end it was decided to proceed with Mullins' direct route over Grosvenor Bridge. The new bridge was designed by F P Sissons and built by Lotz and Keir in 1929.

Fig. 157 West side of Grosvenor Bridge with pipeline. (G M Huggins, 2014)

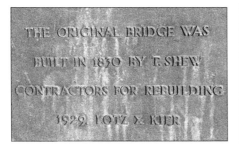

Figs. 158 and 159 Commemorative plaques on Grosvenor Bridge. (G M Huggins, 2014)

After crossing the Grosvenor Bridge the pipeline continued underground; fortunately there was no difficulty when it reached the GWR as the pathway from the bridge passes through an arch under the line at this point. The gravity fed main then started its uphill journey through a small field below the Canal, passing close to the east side of the Folly Public House. Trenches were dug by hand in those days so the workmen may have been glad to

151

enjoy a pint of beer after they finished for the day; they could not have guessed that only a few years later, during World War II, the Inn would be destroyed by a bomb aimed at the railway. Crossing the Canal proved expensive as it had to be drained at a cost of £200 so that the main could be laid under its bed on the eastern side of the Swing Bridge [now replaced by a fixed pedestrian footbridge]. From there the pipeline continued steeply uphill through the Hampton House Paddock to join the Warminster Road.

Fig. 160 The Swing Bridge near The Folly, c1920. (© Bath in Time – Dafnis Collection)

Water from Monkswood, situated on the 380 foot contour, could flow by gravity down the hillside to the valley floor and up the opposite hillside to a maximum height of about 300 feet. At this level a pumping station would have to be built to push the water on up to the new reservoir on the 670 foot high summit of Hampton Down.

As the main had now reached the Warminster Road it was at the height where the pumping station would be needed. Mullins had suggested a site to the south-west behind Nethersole [now King Edward's School] however the Bathwick Estate Company, which owned the land, had plans for a housing development there[52] so this was not practicable. The next site to be considered was to the east in the Trossachs field, but the owner, Miss Reid, was adamant that she would not give consent. A new site, on land belonging to the Golf Club, was soon found about 100 yards further east on the same 285 foot contour and the Council purchased a plot beside the St George's Hill Track for £475. To reach it the main, completed late in 1928, turned left along the Warminster Road, then right to run for a short distance up the track. The Pumping Station and its attendant tank were built by Ernest Ireland of Bath; they finished the pump house in February 1929 and had installed its plant, which could pump 50,000 gallons an hour, by the end of April.

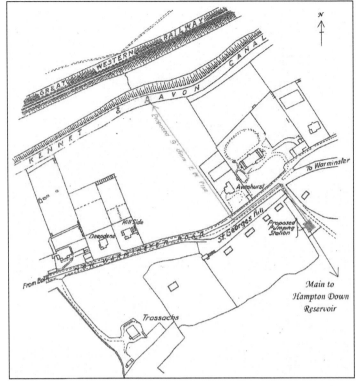

Fig. 161 1928 Plan of overflow pipe (shown red) adapted to show continuation of main from A4 (shown blue). (Bath Record Office)

In addition an overflow pipe from the Pumping Station was laid down to the Warminster Road and continued west of Avonhurst's boundary [now Tasburgh] to empty into the Canal. The Warminster Road Pumping Station is still in use today and can be found immediately behind number 1A St George's Hill.

Coles Bros Ltd, Builders and Civil Engineers of Bath, commenced work on the pipeline from the Pumping Station to Hampton Down in late 1928. A nine inch rising main was laid in a south-easterly direction straight to the reservoir site; the first stretch up through Fussells Wood proved very difficult owing to the steepness of the terrain and the winter weather. The following paraphrases a description of the work involved which appeared in the *Bath Chronicle* of 19 January 1929.

Anyone on the Warminster Road on Wednesday would have seen a *'weird-looking engine climbing the steep, rough track up the side of the hill to the golf links'*. Among the trees was *'a devastated area; brushwood and large stones lay in confusion all around'* where workmen had been busy excavating. The hillside was frozen hard making the task more difficult. The engine, which was making a trial run, was a Fordson Tractor, specially fitted with caterpillar tracks to enable it to make the very steep climb. It was laden with lengths of piping for the new water main which Bath Waterworks Committee is laying to provide the southern slopes of the City with a more adequate supply.

153

Fig. 162 The Warminster Road Pumping Station from the north. (G M Huggins, 2015)

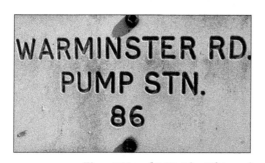

Figs. 163 and 164 Identifying plaques. (G M Huggins, 2015)

The contractors, Messrs Coles Bros, had to solve the problem of getting the pipes, each 9 inches in diameter and weighing 6½ cwt, up the steep slope. Fortunately the vehicle accomplished the task *'with comparative ease'*, driven by Mr Fuller, who had been an officer in charge of such tractors in the war. Once it gained the top of the hill it went *'along to a spot near where the pipes are to be laid and down the slope, of which they will be lowered by means of lines, till they are at the site of the trench in which they are to be placed'*.

After the pipeline left Fussells Wood the task became much easier with the main crossing a field and then three fairways of the Golf Course until it reached its destination. From the London Road to the summit of Hampton Down the workmen had dug 2,452 yards of trenches to lay the inlet main.

The outlet main from the new reservoir had also been completed; it gravitated to the highest levels of Bathwick Hill, Combe Down and Odd Down, with branches off to other upper areas of Bath including Widcombe Hill, Entry Hill and the Wells Road.

The reservoir itself was built by Industrial Construction Ltd of Westminster. Work began in 1928 and severed what was then the 11th hole of the Golf Course[53] [now an area between the 9th green and the 13th tee]. The top of the reservoir was only one foot six inches above ground level and had soil ramped off all around – as there was no fencing cattle could still access the area and grazing rights were unaffected. A hollow 50 yards away was utilised for the tipping of spoil and then grassed over. Building work for the Hampton Down Reservoir scheme was completed late in 1930.

It began operating several months later and on 6 June 1931 the *Bath Chronicle* was able to report that '*The 4,500 consumers in Claverton Down, Combe Down, Odd Down and South Down are now supplied by the new scheme which replaces the supply provided by the Combe Down WW Co. The scheme has taken 2½ years and the actual work of changeover over 6 months. The South Side now gets its water from Monkswood pumped up to the new Hampton Down reservoir by the Warminster Road pumping station. All is satisfactory with no complaints from consumers*'.

The Canal Pumping Station

During the planning for the 1926 South Side Scheme the Bath Council had employed Alex Binnie, Son and Deacon to advise on the proposals. Their report approved the scheme but suggested that an additional main from Monkswood to Lambridge was needed and another large reservoir should be built north of Monkswood at Bull's Hill. However, in October 1929, the Waterworks Committee challenged Binnie's conclusions and in April 1930 the Council abandoned his report and instead looked closely at the way their undertaking had previously been managed. They discovered that although consumption in Bath had remained the same for 20 years there was an increase in water used due to maladministration and waste. Leaking mains had not been repaired and millions of gallons from low level sources at Batheaston, which could be utilised for the south side and prevent strain on unreliable high level sources, were running to waste into the river. The Monkswood main had been tested and had 50% spare capacity so a new main was not necessary, in addition the need for more storage at Bull's Hill was not proved.[54]

By May 1931 the Council voted to supply the south side, via the new Hampton Down Reservoir, from low level sources at a cost of £5,000. This decision was made because the 1926 Scheme was placing demand entirely on the high level supply at Monkswood when more reliable low level sources could provide enough water except in drought conditions. At those times extra water from the high level would be needed.

It is possible that the Councillors' decision was influenced by a talk on unemployment given by the Rt. Hon. J H Thomas, Secretary of State for the Dominions, in Bristol on 27 June 1930. He also spoke of the countrywide water supply problems which had occurred in 1929, the greatest drought period for 100 years, and suggested that building new reservoirs would address both issues as it would create work for a large number of unskilled labourers and increase the water supply. No Local Authority, he said, should have a shortage of water. Although the Council had decided that the Bull's Hill Reservoir was unnecessary their new scheme would address water shortage issues and increase employment opportunities in the Bath area.

The Ministry of Health was also concerned about the state of the nation's water supply and informed the Council in May 1931 that all supplies should be chlorinated if possible; later that year the Council reported that their two main sources of supply had sterilization equipment in place and that it intended to extend it to the others.

By November 1931 the Council's plans to re-organise the supply to the south side were well under way. Unfortunately, the Warminster Road Pumping Station had been built in the wrong place – on the 285 foot contour well above the height of the reservoirs at Oakford and Batheaston at 203 feet and 245 feet respectively. As a result it could not be gravity fed by these low level sources but could only be supplied from Monkswood at the higher level of 380 feet.

Because of this mistake a new, small, pumping station would have to be built at a much lower level on the south bank of the Canal, at the bottom of the Hampton House Paddock, to utilise the surplus low level water. Designed by the City Engineer, F P Sissons, it was to be constructed in brick, faced with Bath Stone, have a flat roof, an underground tank with a capacity of 30,000 gallons and small electric pumps which would increase efficiency and be cheap to run.[55] It would pump water from low level sources directly up to the Hampton Down Reservoir, becoming the main pumping station for supplying the south side of Bath. The Warminster Road Pumping Station would now be a standby, used only when there was a superabundance of water at Monkswood. This scheme would ensure that the south side of the City could be supplied with water from each or all of the available sources in case of need.

On 11 June 1932, the *Bath Chronicle* stated that '*The Warminster Road Pumping Station, put up 2 years ago, will be redundant under the latest scheme*'. The Canal Pumping Station began operating on 2 September that year and three years later the City Engineer reported that the Pumping Machinery at Warminster Road needed repairs. These were not carried out as it was now so infrequently used and the Corporation considered selling the machinery '*if a reasonable offer was received*'. It appears that this did not take place as since then the Pumping Station has been upgraded and is still in use today ensuring that water is delivered to the higher properties in Bathampton and also transferring some water to Bathampton Down Reservoir.

Early in 1942 a three inch pipe was laid from the inlet main immediately below the Canal Pumping Station. It ran westerly through the adjacent 'Steep Field' to supply hutments being erected beside the Warminster Road to house Admiralty office staff moved to Bath for safety early in World War II. Although meant to be temporary these low red brick buildings were still in use until what is now the Ministry of Defence, Navy Department, moved away from Bath several years ago. The old hutments were demolished in 2016 to make way for a housing development.

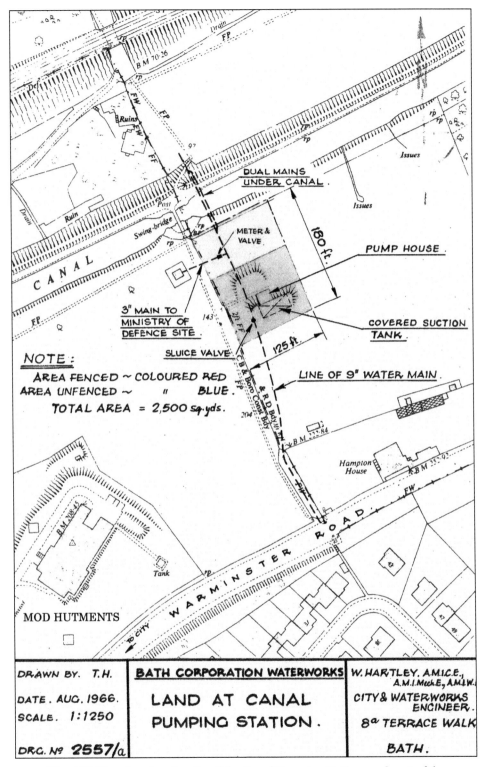

Fig. 165 Plan showing the site of the Canal Pumping Station, and part of the MOD hutments, August 1966. (Bath Record Office)

The Canal Pumping Station was still operating in August 1966 when the Council wished to contact the Misses Thomas, from whom it had bought the site, about unspecified '*proposals concerning the Pumping Station*' and a plan was drawn up, see Fig. 165. As both ladies had died '*the matter was closed*'. At some time after that it became disused and in 1994 Wessex Water made the low level reservoir at Chilcombe Bottom, Batheaston, which had supplied it, operationally redundant and restored it as an area of natural beauty. The derelict building can be seen in Hampton House Paddock beside the canal and has a few remnants of the pumping machinery still in situ.

Fig. 166 Canal Pumping Station. (G M Huggins, 2014)

Figs. 167 and **168** Remains of machinery inside the Pumping Station. (G M Huggins, 2014)

The Bristol, Bath and Mendip Area Water Supply Scheme, 1947-57

As living standards improved after the Second World War people made greater demands on the water supply. The demand for water doubled owing to the increase in housing and better living conditions – consumers expected to have running water and baths in their homes. Industries needed more, for example farms now had modern machinery and needed cleaner, more hygienic milking parlours and good water for the cattle. Water problems which were pressing before the war now became acute; in Bath consumption in 1939 was two million gallons and this was set to almost double over the next 20 years. The City had previously expanded its supply by building new reservoirs at Batheaston in 1848; Monkswood in 1875 and 1890 and Oakford in 1903. It had also constructed another at Midford in 1932, enlarged it in 1944 and taken over the Combe Down Waterworks Company in the same year but this was still not enough to cope with the extra post war demand.

The wartime Coalition Government, looking ahead, passed the Water Act, 1945, which marked the beginning of a national water policy by grouping the numerous local water undertakings into regional areas. It recognised the need for central government to supervise statutory suppliers and be involved in the difficult issues of water supply.

Before the war 24 water authorities were responsible for the supply in the Bristol, Bath and Mendip areas which included parts of Gloucester, Somerset and Wiltshire. Each of these authorities tried to solve their own problems of storage, supply and demand within the limits of their own resources and capital and did not know if they would be able to obtain extra supplies from their neighbours when necessary. The area was fortunate in that, pre 1945, Bristol Waterworks Company had planned a new reservoir in the Chew Valley with a capacity of 4,500 million gallons; work on this started after the war and, after discussion between various authorities (Bristol, West Gloucestershire, Bath and others concerned) Bristol agreed to provide a treatment station at Stowey and maintain the reservoir at Chew on behalf of them all. This provided a water bank on which Bath and the other authorities could draw for supplies.

A decision had to be made on how it was best to get the water to Bath 12 miles away. Various different routes were considered before the best course for the pipeline was finally identified. From the treatment station water was to be pumped up to a new two million gallon reservoir at Clutton; it would then flow seven miles eastwards by gravity to a second reservoir of a similar size at Englishcombe. From there a main would be laid for three miles to join up with the existing distribution system at the Old Bridge, Bath. In September 1952, pipe laying began throughout a cold winter; much of the work was done manually, some was carried out by machines but they were primitive by the standards of the 21st century. Large circular concrete pipe liners had to be used to pass the pipeline under a railway embankment and when crossing streams the cast iron pipes were set in covered ducts to protect them from frost. At the end of the section from Englishcombe to Bath the pipe ran down Holloway towards the Old Bridge [since replaced by the Churchill Bridge, on a slightly different site].

The scheme also included an extension to the existing half million gallon reservoir on Hampton Down, as it was too small for the increased supply needed for the south side of the City. In 1949 plans were drawn up by John Owens, City and Waterworks Engineer, for twin circular reservoirs to be put in on the south side of the Golf Course next to the existing reservoir, sited to avoid two greens and a fairway. Their construction, of reinforced concrete with the walls protected by earth banks to reduce expansion and contraction due to frost or heat, was to be similar to the reservoir at Englishcombe. It was hoped to start work on the new reservoir complex (which would have a capacity of one and a half million gallons and cost about £43,500) in 1951.

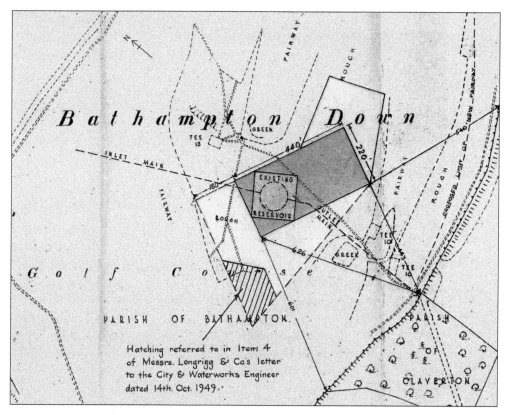

Fig. 169 Plan dated 1950 showing existing 1926 reservoir (blue)
and the proposed extension (red). (Bath Record Office)

The Golf Club were willing to sell the necessary land to the Corporation for £350 subject to several conditions; these included a surrounding fence and screen of trees; moving and widening the 10th fairway; enlarging the 10th tee with excavated soil and moving the ladies tee to the south east. Additionally, they required water to be laid on to the Clubhouse as the supply from the old Combe Down Reservoir often failed. Finally, all surface damage was to be made good and the only access was to be from the south through the gate in the parish boundary wall near the 10th tee. Formerly a wicket gate, this had to be replaced by a 10 foot wide field gate to allow easy access for the contractors and for C G Hancock of Quarry Farm, Claverton Down, the Golf Club's tenant farmer.

The new reservoir complex would not obtain water from Chew Valley but would continue to be supplied by the main from the London Road at Lambridge, plus another main which had been put in later from the Midford Springs. However, a new outlet main to Rush Hill was needed and work on this began at the reservoir in September 1951.

In March 1952 the Ministry of Works noted that the reservoir was to be enlarged and stated that '*It will be necessary for an archaeologist to watch for finds of interest*'. It is not known whether anything was discovered during the building work after a start was made in July 1953 when the Waterworks Engineer made four trenches to evaluate the geology of the area.

Unfortunately the new reservoir site was bisected by the existing bridleway running from the top of Bathwick Hill to Bathampton; this resulted in a considerable delay while various official bodies argued endlessly over the necessary diversion. Meanwhile the contractors, Ernest Ireland & Co had had their tender of £36,000 accepted, were anxious to begin construction and were given permission to do so on 20 October 1954 provided they did not obstruct the bridleway. Eventually the bureaucratic indecision came to an end in 1955 when the obvious solution of a diversion around the western side of the reservoir complex was decided upon. The bridleway still uses this route today, running between the reservoir fence and the surrounding trees.

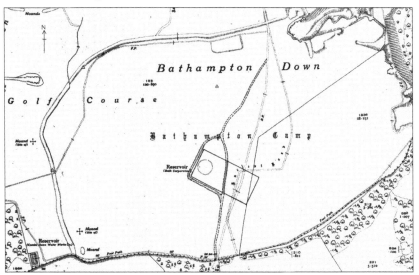

Fig. 170 Plan showing old and new bridleway routes, 1955. (Bath Record Office)

Fig. 171 The bridleway skirting the south-western corner of the reservoir fence. (M F Clark, 2016)

161

Irelands began work on Hampton Down by excavating and levelling the site before a concrete floor was laid in sections. In February 1955 the Golf Club raised several concerns *'Contractors are from time to time blasting on the site and several pieces of rock and stone have fallen on the 12th green while members were playing there. Blasting should take place when players are not on the course'* and *'the temporary roadway to the site is in bad condition, cut up by lorries and machinery'.*

A further problem arose when a geological fault was uncovered during the excavation. It ran across the site of one of the twin reservoirs, varying in width from 12 inches to 18 inches, and had to be bridged with reinforced concrete before the floor could be laid. The walls, made of concrete sections which held the water in by ring tension, similar to that of a barrel, were then erected and rows of pillars with enlarged fluted tops put in across the floor ready to support the roof. Lastly, a chamber was constructed between the two circular reservoirs to house the control valves and recording equipment and the pipework of the existing reservoir was interconnected so that all three could be controlled at this single point. All the reservoirs could work as one as they were the same size with a top water level of 670 feet above sea level and a depth of ten feet.

The roof, made of reinforced concrete slabs, could now be put on. Heaps of spoil from the excavation were used to embank the reservoir walls and the whole construction was then covered with earth and sown with grass seed so that it would blend in with the landscape. Only the valve chamber *'of a pleasing design'* showed. As Irelands finished each stage of the work at Hampton Down their men and machinery were transferred to work on constructing the very similar reservoir at Englishcombe.

On 14 October 1955 the *Bath Chronicle* reported that *'Hampton Down Reservoir is 58% completed and should be ready for service next January. It will eventually appear as a tree surrounded hill'.* As the bridleway diversion had now been settled the conveyance of the land from the Golf Club to Bath Corporation could proceed at last and took place on 24 June 1957. By then farmer Hancock had relinquished his rights to cut hay on the reservoir area, a six foot fence had been erected around it and the requested screen of trees planted.

The Chew Valley Lake had been opened in 1956 and the whole Mendip Scheme was completed in 1957. As a result Bath's water supply was increased tenfold to over 600 million gallons. A film *Water for a City* was made to illustrate the works carried out by Bath Corporation from the scheme's inception in 1947 to its completion ten years later.

On 1 April 1958, the Mayor of Bath, his Council Members and Chief Officials plus representatives of the other Councils involved received invitations from Councillor Mannings to a viewing at the Pump Room followed by afternoon tea at 4.30. There was also a free screening for members of the public on the following Wednesday. A copy of this film can be viewed at the Bristol Record Office and provides a fascinating and invaluable record of the construction of this enormous undertaking, including the building of the two additional reservoir chambers on Hampton Down.[56]

Fig. 172 Excavating the site

Fig. 173 Constructing a chamber

Fig. 174 Putting on the roof

Fig. 175 Final stages

From the 1957 film *Water for a City*, F G Warne Collection. (Bristol Record Office Ref. BROFA/0144)

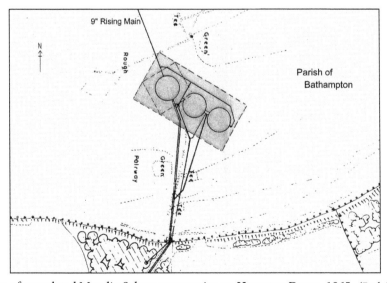

Fig. 176 Plan of completed Mendip Scheme reservoirs on Hampton Down, 1965. (Bath Record Office)

The Bathampton Meadows Scheme

It had been thought that the Bristol, Bath and Mendip Scheme would ensure an adequate supply for Bath until at least 1970, but increasing consumption during the 1950s and the dry summer of 1959 revealed that this would not be the case. Consumption in Bath and throughout the country was outstripping previous estimates and in January 1960 Bristol Waterworks enquired whether Bath was going to need more water from them. As a result, only three years after the Mendip Scheme was completed, the Bath City Engineer investigated a possible new source at Bathampton Meadows. This would use a new method of extracting water from shallow gravels, and would be a cheaper option than an extra supply from Bristol.

Twelve and a half acres would be needed in meadows situated next to the river on Bathampton Farm, owned by George Albert Glass. There followed a tortuous and long drawn out process of planning, investigation and negotiation with the farmer. During this time he made several claims for compensation for damage to his land and at one point the Corporation considered buying the farm outright as, owing to legal problems, it was proving difficult to buy the area in question alone. Then the British Transport Commission became involved over rights of way to the farm over a level crossing. Mr Glass had been using it to access his caravan site rather than for agricultural purposes and on 9 December 1963 the Commission took him to court over this, however the judge ruled that such access was not illegal and he won the case. Next the GWR made objections to the scheme over fears that abstraction near the railway line could cause problems.

The whole saga dragged on from 1959, when the Corporation began negotiations to buy the land, until July 1964. At that point the contract with Mr Glass was ready to be signed when the Corporation suddenly pulled out, resulting in a generous payment of compensation to the farmer. Another site for extraction had been found, west of the City at Newton Meadows, this would yield a far better supply – four million gallons per day instead of just under one million gallons at Bathampton. The Newton Meadows abstraction scheme went ahead, opening in 1969, and is still operating today.

Extension to Hampton Down Reservoir 1967-70

In 1965, just after the decision on the Newton Meadows Scheme was made, the Corporation also began planning to increase their supply to the south side of the City. Consumption for that area was expected to rise to forty per cent of the total for the whole Bath district by 1972, owing to the proposed new University, the concentration of Navy Department staff at the Foxhill hutments and more housing developments. The Hampton Down Reservoir would have to be extended by adding an extra 'wing' built at a slight angle to the west end of the existing reservoirs to form an open 'V' shape. More water was required to fill this new chamber but the Tucking Mill and Midford sources were already pumping to their limit and it was impractical to increase the size of the main from Monkswood. The solution was to build a pumping station beside the Englishcombe Reservoir with a new main running to the Red Lion at Odd Down. From that point water which had originated at the Chew Valley

Lake could continue along the existing Midford main to the Hampton Down Reservoir.

Planning then began for the new pumping station, main and reservoir. In December 1965 the Ministry of Public Building and Works wrote to the Corporation asking if it had any objections to the scheduling of parts of Bathampton and Claverton Downs as an ancient monument, the area involved being mainly the Iron Age enclosure. The Council replied that they did not as long as their plans to construct another reservoir adjacent to the existing one could go ahead. The Ministry agreed to this and the scheduling took place in 1966.

Fig. 177 Aerial view, looking west, showing the inverted 'V' shape of reservoirs 1 to 4 surrounded by the Celtic Field System. (West Air Photography, 1976)

The Golf Club were not informed of the Corporation's plan until 1967 when they received a request for land on which to extend the reservoir *'to cope with a two million gallon requirement for the new University'.*[57] Built on Claverton Down on fields which had belonged to Norwood Farm the new Campus was sited close to the south side of the Claverton/ Bathampton parish boundary wall, a short distance from the reservoir. It can be seen top left in the above illustration. Bath University opened in 1966 with a first intake of 1,260 students. Fifty years on it has over 16,000 students and its buildings have spread to cover a large, roughly triangular area bordered by the Bathampton/Claverton boundary wall on the north, Bushy Norwood to the east and Claverton Down Road to the south.

The Golf Club agreed to sell the land for the new reservoir for the sum of £2,000, the conveyance was signed in December 1968 and excavation was being carried out by March of the following year. By the end of 1969 the concrete structure had been completed and was being tested; only the embankments and surface works had to be finished. These were in place by 3 March 1970 when new fencing was being erected around the site and the Hampton Reservoir No. 4 came into service by 5 May despite serious problems with the new main from Englishcombe due to numerous joint failures.

In 1971 it was found that water was running to waste from the Midford spring; in order to utilise this the Corporation planned to transport it via a new main to Tucking Mill where water from both places would be treated and pumped through a new rising main to Hampton Down. The whole scheme would cost £94,000. In the summer of 1972 work began on the new mains; these were completed a year later together with a new reservoir at Tucking Mill.

Today the Hampton Down Reservoir is supplied by a variety of sources; primarily the springs at Tucking Mill and Midford which draw water from both high and low level sources. It also receives water from the Englishcombe Reservoir which in turn is supplied from borehole sources in Wiltshire's Wylye Valley and with water imported from Wessex Water's neighbouring company Bristol Water; there is also a very small supply from the Warminster Road Pumping Station.

Fig. 178 Nameplate at gateway to the reservoirs. (M F Clark, 2015)

Fig. 179 Gates to reservoirs. (M F Clark, 2014)

Source Reservoirs

The following illustrations show Monkswood, which was the original water supply to Hampton Down Reservoir, and the Chew Valley Lake, the major source for the Mendip Scheme.

Fig. 180 The opening ceremony of Monkswood Reservoir, 8 June 1897, from the *Bath and County Graphic*. (Bathwick LHS Archive)

Fig. 181 Chew Valley Lake with control tower and dam. (Google Images, 2008)

Wessex Water

In 1974 the UK water industry was nationalised and the Wessex Water Authority formed to serve a population of around two million people living in Wiltshire, Somerset, Dorset and Gloucestershire. Locally it took over all responsibility for water supply and sewerage disposal from the Bath Corporation, including the Hampton Down Reservoirs. In 1989 all the UK water boards were privatised and Wessex Water was formed to purchase the assets of the Wessex Water Authority. More recently (2002) Wessex Water was bought by a Malaysian conglomerate, YTL Power International of Kuala Lumpur; however it has retained the name of Wessex Water and still operates in the West Country including Bath and the surrounding area. Its head office is now sited on the Claverton Down Road only a mile or two from Hampton Down.

The Television Masts

Just before the reservoir was extended one other major project, unconnected to the water industry, took place on the hilltop. In July 1965 the BBC approached the Golf Club with a request to purchase a piece of land on the Warren in order to erect a television mast. There was much opposition from the local community as many people thought it would be a blot on the landscape. However, after much deliberation the Club Committee agreed to sell a plot outside the course boundary, adjacent to the third tee, for the sum of £1,000.

The original mast has since been heightened and a second mast erected on the same plot in 1995. They form a prominent, if somewhat ugly feature on the skyline, which can be clearly seen from miles around, but does have the merit of being a landmark which clearly identifies Bathampton Down.

Fig. 182 The Communication masts on Bathampton Down. (G M Huggins, 2015)

POSTSCRIPT

The use of Bath Stone on the Down

Fig. 183 William Harbutt, the inventor of Plasticene, with his children
Olive and Noel (with telescope) on Hampton Down, 1886.
This stone walled track cannot be identified.
(W Mannings – Harbutt Collection)

STONE GATE-POSTS, STILES AND CURIOS

The local 'Bath' stone has been put to good use for centuries on Hampton Down for building walls. It has also provided larger blocks for use as gateposts and stiles, many of which have probably been in use since long before Allen's time. The following pictures serve as a record of those still in evidence in 2017 together with other little known curios not covered elsewhere in this publication.

Gateposts

The present bridleway follows the route of an ancient trackway, once referred to as 'Downs Lane', which led from the village up to Hampton Down and across the plateau to Claverton Down. It is marked at either end of the Down by large stone gate posts which abut the present gateways.

Fig. 184 Stone gate post on 'Downs Lane' as the ancient way leads onto Hampton Down. The arch under the wall, now silted up, once took the overspill of spring water on its way to the village. (G M Huggins, 2016)

As the way climbs up the slope it is extremely worn and cuts deeply into the hillside. It has, no doubt, been used since the Iron Age when early occupants living near the flood plain in the valley below made their way up to their enclosure on the plateau. It not only gave access to the hilltop for their successors but formed an important link in a series of routes leading south-westwards. It would have been used by carts carrying loads of stone down to the village, in particular for the upkeep of the parish roads, and was also a route taken by the thousands of race-goers on their way to the racecourse on Claverton Down during the 18th century.

Fig. 185 Looking down the ancient way towards the gateway. (G M Huggins, 2016)

In 1966 Bath University was built across the direct route of the bridleway which ran from Hampton Down to the top of Bathwick Hill. As a result the ancient track was diverted two ways and now circumnavigates the campus on either side. A short section of the original way can still be found immediately south of the boundary wall and is used to access the nearby Bathampton Down Reservoir. It has also been used by farmers who have an agreement to cut the rough beside the Golf Course for hay.

Fig. 186 The stone gate post (from the north) where the ancient way left Hampton Down and entered Claverton Down. (M F Clark, 2011)

Fig. 187 Another stone gate post leads from 'Downs Lane' into field numbered 51 (see Fig. 25). It still contains lead used for fixing hinges.
(G M Huggins, 2015)

A pair of stone gateposts still marks the point where the old quarry track from Single Way Mine passed into Sham Castle Field, just east of Sham Castle, en route to the North Road.

Fig. 188 Gate posts where the track from Single Way Mine entered Sham Castle Field – looking south-west.
(See also Fig. 76).
(G M Huggins, 2014)

Spring Markers

The spring marker post to the west of Sham Castle may well have had other uses before being utilized by the Bath City Waterworks (see also Fig. 131 and pages 128-129). Bath Stone was also used for many other spring markers to be found in the fields and woods below Sham Castle in the parish of Bathwick.

Fig. 189 East side of the spring marker post at Sham Castle recording site of 'Bath City Waterworks No. 14' spring. (See also Fig. 131).
(G M Huggins, 2014)

Stone Stiles

Stone stiles feature widely throughout the British countryside and no more so than in the Cotswolds where stone is plentiful. They provided an easy means of access on ancient rights of way between field boundaries or parishes. Their style varies within regions much depending on the type of stone available but they were normally constructed to deny access by animals. Bathampton has a number of excellent examples most of which are found on the Down. There are three such stiles set in the wall which marks the parish boundary as it runs around the southern and western extremes of Sham Castle Field. The first of these is immediately south-west of Sham Castle where a footpath leads into the parish of Bathwick and onto Golf Club Road.

Fig. 190 Stone stile set in the boundary wall immediately south-west of Sham Castle, viewed from east.
(G M Huggins, 2014)

Fig. 191 The stile shown in Fig. 190 viewed from west. (G M Huggins, 2015)

The second stile, in the south-western corner of the field leads into Bathwick and North Road. It lay buried for a number of years in undergrowth but was reinstated during the winter of 2015-16 by students from Bath University in conjunction with the National Trust. The immediate sections of the boundary wall were also rebuilt.

Fig. 192 Reinstated stone stile set in boundary wall in south-west corner of Sham Castle Field, north side.
(M F Clark, 2016)

Fig. 193 Reinstated stile, south side.
(M F Clark, 2016)

175

The third is set in the boundary wall between Bathampton and Bath University Campus. Beside the stile is a marker post which is now virtually indecipherable, although the upper line may read 'L' and 'B' and the lower line appears to be a 'V' or 'W' followed by a further 'W'.

In 1938 A V Gandy wrote of an excursion to find the stone marking the Duel. She records the above lettering as 'E' 'B' 'V' 'W' and adds that the *humourist of the party* translated this as '*Edward. Barry. Valiantly. Wounded*', however '*as the victim's name was Jean Baptiste that stone had to be ruled out*'.[1] The stone is positioned where the three parishes of Bathampton, Claverton and Bathwick once met, but this offers little in solving the meaning of the lettering or the mystery of the missing Duel stone.

Fig. 194 Stone stile (from the east) in the boundary wall, south-east corner of Sham Castle Field, with inscribed marker stone set in adjoining wall. (G M Huggins, 2014)

Fig. 195 Close-up of marker stone, now virtually indecipherable. (G M Huggins, 2014)

Following the boundary wall on around Sham Castle field to where it delineates the southern edge of the Golf Course there is a further stile made of a single stone 'slab' which is set in the southern most part of the wall (see also Fig. 95 and pages 94-95). A section of this, next to the stile, was demolished to allow the bridleway to pass through when it was diverted westwards from the Golf Course onto Bath University Campus some years ago.

Fig. 196 Stone 'Slab' stile adjacent to the bridleway, south side.
(G M Huggins, 2016)

Fig. 197 'Slab' stile and bridleway from the north looking towards the University campus.
(M F Clark, 2013)

There are several stone stiles on Claverton Down but only one other stile on Bathampton Down. It stands to the north of the site of the former Bathampton Waterworks tank on a footpath which leads up from the Warminster Road. Wooden 'cross bars' were reinstated by the Cotswold Wardens some years ago but sadly only the upright stone supporting posts with their slotted housings now stand.

Fig. 198 Remains of stile immediately north of the old Bathampton Waterworks tank, viewed from the south. (G M Huggins, 2014)

Remains of the extensive quarry workings

The numerous stone outcrops and remains of extensive quarry workings that line the eastern slopes of the Down gave rise to the area becoming known as 'Hampton Rocks'.

Today the whole area, which was once bare and open, has completely changed as it has become covered by trees and bushes. It is still possible to explore this mysterious world of a bygone age; however it is dangerous in many places due to the instability of the old workings.

Fig. 199 Typical view of old quarry workings on east side of Bathampton Down. (G M Huggins, 2014)

Fig. 200 One of the many stone stacks to be found amongst the old quarry workings.
(G M Huggins, 2014)

Agriculture

As already mentioned, the extensive prehistoric remains on the Down[2] with the outlines of numerous small fields dating back to the Iron Age, give evidence of early agricultural practices, but there is now little trace of recent activities. There are, however, two pieces of machinery which were used in a more modern agricultural age that can still be found lying abandoned in undergrowth on the plateau.

Fig. 201 A hay rake alongside the underground reservoir. (G M Huggins, 2009)

Fig. 202 Equipment near the Iron Age enclosure. (G M Huggins, 2009)

Other Curios

On the level below the Devil's Table can be found a large stone with the following curious carving on its north face. It became known as 'The Altar Stone' by the Bathampton Scouts in the 1930s-40s when they used it as a meeting point during patrol exercises on the hillside.

Fig. 203 The 'Altar' Stone. (G M Huggins, 2014)

The remaining 'Dry Arch' of the Inclined Plane, which is situated just above the Warminster Road, contains a good deal of graffiti but nothing quite so scary as the skull shown below.

Fig. 204 The 'skull' carved into the side of the remaining arch. (G M Huggins, 2014)

Another curious remnant on the Down is the following arch which is found built into the southern boundary wall just east of the 'slab' stile. The remains of the wall on either side of it are straight sided, as though marking a form of gateway. The arch is supported by these two sides but the space below has been subsequently in-filled.

Its purpose is a mystery. It could have been the means of allowing sheep to feed on either side of the wall at a time when, during the 17th and 18th centuries, both Bathampton and Claverton Manors were held by the Lord of Claverton Manor – the arch preventing large animals following suit. A less likely possibility is that it was built to accommodate the roots of a large tree.

Fig. 205 The curious arch in the southern parish boundary
wall, viewed from the south. (G M Huggins, 2016)

Near the Devil's Table is not only the Devil's Cave but also the Devil's Chimney. The
'Chimney' is formed by a large stone slab lying on its side forming a 'passageway' giving
enough room to crawl through from one side to another. Part of it has a small fissure which
allows warm air from the caverns below to escape into the atmosphere. This appears as a
mist (condensation) when the air above ground is colder than that rising from below. Often
thought, mistakenly, as being smoke – hence the name. There are many such occurrences
on the Down which, given the right conditions, have on numerous occasions resulted in
tales of ghosts having been seen.

Fig. 206 Stone stacks near Devil's Table with Bathford in the distance, c1920.
(© Bath in Time – Dafnis Collection)

There is no doubt as to which cave is that named the Devil's Cave as on one of the remaining stone faces someone has gone to great trouble in painting the Devil himself!

Fig. 207 The 'Devil' in Devil's Quarry.
(Courtesy of David Grosvenor, 2010)

AUTHOR'S NOTES

I had the good fortune to grow up in Bathampton during the 1940s and 50s – a time when it was still a relatively quiet country village. Children were free to 'go out to play' and explore their surroundings, unhindered by today's volume of traffic and fear of strangers – our parents did not worry as long as we were home 'in time for tea'. Our playground was Bathampton Down, where we could climb the steep hillside to the Rocks, peer inside the caves left by the quarrymen, slide down stony scree slopes, collect fossils, watch tiny lizards basking in the sun and lay on our stomachs on the highest point of all looking down to the valley below. Unlike today, the old quarries were almost bare of trees and shrubs, so our view was unimpeded.

I lived at 13 St George's Hill, some distance from the centre of the village. My parents' house, perched high above the Warminster Road, had extensive views towards Little Solsbury at the front and a long, narrow garden running steeply up the hillside at the back. In the hedge at the top my father had made a small gate; this gave access to the large field behind the houses, which was typical of the open pastures occupying the lower slopes of the Down at that time. Once called 'The Mount' it was very steep on the north-eastern side but less so to the south-west.

Fig. 208 Top of garden with field beyond, 1951.   **Fig. 209** In the field with giant mushroom, 1950.

Probably because of the terrain it had never been ploughed so was full of a great variety of grasses and wild flowers. In spring there were cowslips, spires of purple orchids and the row of great elms in the hedgerow at the bottom of the field was covered in a dull mist of pink blossom. In summer a patch of bee orchids often appeared near the bog at the south-western end. Each year it produced something to marvel at, a crop of giant horse mushrooms, puffballs, fairy rings, or a long tailed tits nest in a bramble bush, amazingly constructed of pieces of lichen with a domed top and small entrance hole at the front. It was a haven for wildlife, the chiffchaff and cuckoo heralded spring and warblers could be seen as well as the more usual garden birds. By day there was the sound of grasshoppers chirping in chorus and care was needed not to step on a grass snake basking in the sun. At night one was often woken by the hooting of an owl or the scream of a vixen.

Sadly, what I once regarded as 'my' field is now completely overgrown with trees and scrub which make the area inaccessible and unrecognisable as the place where I used to play. My mother foresaw this – she realised that because the encroaching brambles at the sides of the field were no longer cleared they provided a place for saplings to grow, safe from grazing cattle. When these trees matured the bushes below would die off – the area eventually turning to woodland. This is exactly what has happened. Fussells Wood, however, which bordered the north-eastern side of the field, is still much the same. This was another favourite spot where one could dam streams, build dens, collect firewood, run through the carpet of white wood anemones in spring, take home bunches of bluebells for mother and climb hazel trees to enjoy the soft, sweet kernels of the early nuts in autumn. Best of all was making a fire in a ring of stones and cooking sausages in an old frying pan.

On Sunday afternoons I enjoyed long walks over the Downs with my parents, Ron and Flo Urch. It was a popular place where families came out from Bath to picnic and made fires in the old quarries and on the nearby slopes. However, during winter it was not always possible to access the Down from our house as a wet season could make climbing the steep, muddy hillside too difficult. Bad weather also caused problems during the summer of 1968 when, on the 10 July, the worst storm for 50 years hit the north Somerset area causing serious flooding at Pensford and Keynsham. Five inches of torrential rain fell in less than 24 hours; by nightfall the Down could absorb no more and water began to pour down the hillside above the Warminster Road. Torrents of water ran down through our back garden, washing away much of the topsoil; it did not get into the house thanks to my father, who was up all night sweeping it away from the back door.

Although material things were in short supply after the war we children had something far better – independence and the freedom to explore Bathampton Down which provided so much to interest and enjoy. My happy childhood memories and interest in the local history of the parish inspired me to write this book for the Group. It seemed important not only to record the more recent history of the hill but also to set down what it was like before further changes take place. Every effort has been made to ensure accuracy but the Bathampton Local History Research Group would welcome comments and any further information.

Lastly I would like to thank my friend, Gillian Huggins, who has done an immense amount of hard work helping me to produce this book. I could not possibly have done so without all her patient, cheerful help and support. Grateful thanks also to my husband, Terry, for his input and my daughter, Cath Field, for assisting so ably with the maps and plans.

Fig. 210 Riding Gypsy, with Gill on Violet, in St George's Hill, 1959.

Mary Clark (née Urch)
June 2017

184

Abbreviations used in this publication

Bathwick LHS	Bathwick Local History Society
BCL	Bath Central Library
BLHRG	Bathampton Local History Research Group
BNA	British Newspaper Archive
BRO	Bath Record Office
BrRL	Bristol Reference Library
BrRO	Bristol Record Office
BRLSI	Bath Royal Literary and Scientific Institute
coll.	Collection
nd.	No date
op. cit.	As previously cited
rep.	Reprint
rev. ed.	Revised Edition
SA&LSS	Somerset Archives and Local Studies Service (Somerset Heritage Centre)
VAG	Victoria Art Gallery, Bath
WHC	Wiltshire History Centre

References and Sources

Foreword
References:
1. Rod Thomas, *A Sacred Landscape – The Prehistory of Bathampton Down.* (Millstream Books, 2008).

Introducing Bathampton Down
References:
1. *A Survey of the Manours of Hampton, Claverton with Widcombe belonging to Ralph Allen, Esq., c1740-64.* Generally referred to as 'Ralph Allen's Estate Map'. (BRO Acc. No. 028/854).

Charles Holder's Wall
References:
1. Decresale [Decree] Order, dated 6 May 1734, Charles Holder v James Charmbury. (BLHRG Ref. Nos 45 and 48).
2. From *A Guide to the Estates of Ralph Allen* by Mike Chapman. Published by The Survey of Old Bath, 2007.
3. John Rhodes, *Bath Golf Club – A History.* Publisher unknown, 2000.

PART ONE
Bathampton Warren
References:
1. From *A Survey of the Mannor of Bathwick in the County of Somerset belonging to the Hon. William Pulteney Esq., taken 1727.* (© British Library Board, Maps K.Top 37. 29a).
2. Somerset Quarter Sessions Records. (SA&LSS Ref. Q\SR/300/223-224 and Q\SR/301/9-11).
3. *The Life of Richard Jones* Transcription from mss with introduction by C. G. 1838 (BCL)
4. All reports of court cases were taken from the *Bath Weekly Chronicle.* (BNA).

Other Sources:
Tom Williamson, *The Archaeology of Rabbit Warrens.* Shire Publications Ltd., 2006.

Murder at the Warren House

References:
1. Lyncombe and Widcombe Parish Register 1574-1772. (SA&LSS, Ref. D\P\wid/2/1/12).
2. Lyncombe and Widcombe Vestry Minutes 1732-54 pp 157 and 159. (SA&LSS, Ref. D\P\wid/9/1/2).

Other Sources:
James Tunstall, *Rambles around Bath*. 2nd edition, 1848. (BCL).
Bath and County Graphic 1898-99, Extract from the Old Ferry Steps. (BCL).
The Bath Journal, 20 June 1748 to 5 June 1749. (BCL).
Gentleman's Magazine, 14 Sept 1748. (Internet).
General Advertiser, 20 September 1748. (Internet).
Bath Chronicle, 22 May 2006. (BCL).

A Time of Change : the Impact of Ralph Allen

References:
1. Entitled *A Survey of the Manours of Hampton, Claverton with Widcombe belonging to Ralph Allen Esqr.*, but generally referred to as 'Ralph Allen's Estate Map'. Undated but believed to have been gradually compiled between 1740 and 1764. (BRO Acc. No. 028/854).
2. *The Life of Richard Jones* transcription from MSS with introduction by C. G. 1838. (BCL).
3. Marjorie Williams, *Lady Luxborough goes to Bath*. Blackwell, 1945. (BRO).
4. www.sandersonmiller.com/architectural - catalogue1 - pdf
5. William Pulteney's Survey of the Manor of Bathwick, 1727, enclosure No. 85. (Copy courtesy of BathwickLHS).
6. Edmund Rack, *Survey of Somerset, 1781*. Section 32, Claverton.
7. Trevor Fawcett, *Georgian Imprints*.
8. *John Weeks' Scrapbook* c1819. (BrRL).
9. *Bath & County Graphic*, July 1902, p33. (BCL).
10. Bath & NES Terrier, ST 255430 Deeds, Batch No. 434, Packet No. 3087. (BRO).

Other Sources:
Various reports from the *Bath Chronicle* and *Bath Journal* 1814-1921. (BCL).

Queen's College

Other Sources:
The *Bath Weekly Chronicle* between 1.11.1838 and 20.8.1840. (BNA).
Prospectus of Queen's College, Bath. (BCL, Ref. 1102987550 and 1102602655).
Bathwick Tithe Map and Schedule, c1838. (SA&LSS Ref. D\D\Rt/M/176).

The Forgotten Farmstead

References:
1. General Register Office, Southampton:
Index of Births – William King [3rd child] registered June Quarter 1867 at St George's Hanover Square [London].
Birth certificate – Claude King [4th child] 26 June 1869, place of birth Bathampton.
2. John Rhodes, *Bath Golf Club – A History*. 2000. Publisher unknown, 2000.
3. OS Sheet XIV 6, 1885. (BRO).

The Golf Course

References:
1. During its early years the course was described in the Club Minutes and the *Bath Chronicle* as 'the Links'. Today this term is generally used to describe a course which runs alongside the sea.
2. The tenancy agreement was retained by the Candy family.
3. *Bath Weekly Chronicle*, 22 March, 1913. (BCL).
4. The labels are held by Bath Central Library and can also be seen on Bath in Time No. 17571.

Other Sources :

John Rhodes, *Bath Golf Club – A History*. Publisher unknown, 2000.
Robert H K Browning, *The Bath Golf Club, Sham Castle*. London Golf Clubs Association, 1929. (BCL).
The Bath Golf Club Official Handbook. Derby New Centurion Publishing, c1947. (BCL).
Bath Golf Club Official Handbook. Published by E G Brown, Bristol c1984. (BLHRG).
Bath Golf Club Official Brochures 2013 and 2014. Publisher unknown. (BLHRG).

PART TWO
Quarries and Quarrying
Section I, Winning the Stone

References:
1. John Wood, *Essay towards a description of Bath*. W Frederick, rev. ed. 1749. (BCL).
2. *The Life of Richard Jones*. Transcription with introduction by C. G. 1858. (BCL).
3. Bob Whittaker, May 2005.
4. David Pollard, November 2012.
5. *Somerset Archaeological Society's Proceedings*, 1877-79, 'Mediaeval Deeds of Bath and District'. Vol. 23, p81. (BRO).
6a. Neice, not sister, ref. Holder wills and Conveyance of 1745. (BLHRG)
6. Court Books including the Manor of Bathampton belonging to William Button Esq., 1560-64. (SA&LSS Ref. DD\WHb/3099).
7. R E M Peach, *The Life and Times of Ralph Allen of Prior Park, Bath*. D Nutt, 1895. (BCL).
8. Sir Arthur Elton, 'The Pre-History of Railways'. *Proceedings of the Somerset Archaeological and Natural History Society*, 1962-63. (BCL).
9. Plan of the Proposed Variation and Extension Lines of the Kennet and Avon Canal, 1797. (SA&LSS Ref. Q\RUP/15).
10. Frederick Shum, 'Some Notes on Gainsborough and His Connection with Bradford'. *Wiltshire Archaeological and Natural History Magazine* XX, 1882. (Wiltshire and Swindon Archives), and, Henry Venn Lansdown, *Recollections of the late William Beckford*. 1840. Rep. by Bath Kingsmead Reprints, c1970. (BCL).
11. The Farrington Diary, 20 September 1806 – 8 January 1808. (Internet – site removed).
12. Bathampton Highway Accounts, 1784-1831. (SA&LSS Ref. D\P\bahton/14/5/1).
13. Edmund Rack, *Survey of Somerset, 1781-87*. Published by Somerset Archaeological Society, 2011. (BCL).
14. Valuation of the Manor of Bathampton 1787-88. (BRO Ref. 371/1).
15. Allen Family Papers – Leases. (BRO Ref. 33/16 Stone, King and Wardle).
16. Sir Arthur Elton, 'The Pre-History of Railways'. *Proceedings of the Somerset Archaeological and Natural History Society*, 1963. (BCL).

Other Sources:

Peter Addison, *Around Combe Down*. Millstream Books, 1998.
J W Perkins, A T Brooks and A E McR Pearce, *Bath Stone, a Quarry History*. 1979.

Quarries and Quarrying
Section II, Transportation: the Tramway

References:
17. C Von Oeynhausen and H Von Dechen, *Railways in England 1826 and 1827*. Translated by E A Forward. Newcomen Society, 1971. (M F Clark).
18. The National Archives Ref. RAIL 842/10.
19. *Bath Guide* dated 1809. (BCL).
20. David Pollard, 'Bath Stone Quarry Railways 1795-1830'. *Bristol Industrial Archaeological Society Journal*, 1982. (BCL).
21. P J G Ransom, *The Archaeology of Railways*. 1935. (BCL).
22. Pierce Egan, *Walks through Bath*. Meylor and Son, 1819. (BCL).

Quarries and Quarrying
Section III, Decline and Closure

References:
23. *The Gentleman's Magazine*, Dec – June 1824, Vol. 94. (BCL).
24. Allen Family Papers – Leases. (BRO Ref. 33/16 Stone, King and Wardle).
25. James Tunstall, *Rambles about Bath and its neighbourhood*. 2nd ed. William Pocock, 1848.
26. David Pollard, November 2012.
27. Lease of 6 June, 1855, Lord William Powlett to Ralph S Allen Esq. (BRO Ref. 0036/23/1).
28. Advertisement, *Bath Chronicle*, 22 November, 1877. (BNA).
29. John Rhodes, *Bath Golf Club – A History*. Publisher unknown, 2000.
30. Back row: - - -; - Jesseman; two Bathampton girls. Middle row: Emily Jesseman, sister of Charlotte Netherwood; Charlotte Netherwood; Margaret Netherwood; Nelly Netherwood; Dudley Jesseman. Front Row: Bessie Netherwood niece of Charlotte; George Netherwood.
31. *Bath Weekly Chronicle*, 2 September 1961, and, *Bath Daily Chronicle*, 6 November 1961. (BCL).
32. D Irwin and A Jarrett, *Mendip Underground, a Cavers Guide*. 1997 ed. and 4th rev. ed. 1999. (SA&LSS).

Death of a Viscount : a Famous Duel

References:
1. Jean Baptiste du Barré was born in 1749, the eldest child of the Count of Cerés. He married Mademoiselle de Touron in 1773. They had one child who died in infancy.
2. Pierce Egan, *Walks through Bath*. Meyler & Son at The Bath Herald, 1819. (BCL).
3. Various reports on Claverton Down in the *Bath Chronicle* 1770-99. (BCL).
4. Report on the trial of Count Rice, *Bath Chronicle*, 8 April 1779. (BCL).
5. *Bath Chronicle* Notes and Queries, 1935. (BCL).
6. Letters to the *Bath Chronicle* and author from Phil Urch, February – May 2007. (BCL).
7. Peter Addison, *Around Combe Down*. Millstream Books, 1998. (BCL).

Other Sources:
Original reports on the Duel and the inquest in the *Bath Chronicle & Weekly Gazette*, 26 November 1778. (BCL).
An early, undated account by the Duke of Northumberland's Chaplain, a close friend of the du Barré's, published in the *Bath Natural History & Antiquarian Field Club Magazine*, Vol III, 1877. (BCL).

The Rifle Range

Other Sources:
Various reports from the *Bath Chronicle* 1860-72. (BNA).
The Skrine Papers. (SA&LSS Ref. DD\SK/5/2 and DD\SK/5/14).
John Rhodes, *Bath Golf Club – A History*. Publisher unknown, 2000.
R Scammell, *14th Warleigh Manor Rifle Volunteer Corps*. (www.bathfordsociety.org.uk).

The Hampton Rocks Mystery

References:
1. Mr John Fudge (born 1897) to Miss Rosemary Dyer, and, *Bath Chronicle*, Monday, 22 October 1973 – interview with Leonard Snell of The Normans, Bathampton.
2. Harry Patch, *The Last Fighting Tommy*. Bloomsbury Publishing, 2008. Also oral record between Mrs F Urch (born 1906) and Mrs M F Clark.
   Harry Patch says the cross commemorated the duel of 1778, this is unlikely so long after the event.
   Mrs Urch saw it near the quarry edge where Elsie was murdered c20 years after the event and said it was in Elsie's memory, this seems the most likely explanation.
3. *Bath Chronicle*, 25 August, 1928. (BCL).

Other Sources:
The Times and *Bath Chronicle* between 25 September, 1893 and 1 March, 1894. (Times Archive, BNA and BCL).

A Wartime Secret : the Bathampton Auxiliary Unit Patrol

References:
1. www.coleshillhouse.com/bob.millard.php

From Rainfall to Reservoirs
Section I, Springs arising on Bathampton Down

References:
1. Verbal evidence from Michael Melksham of Bathampton, 2014.
2. Marek Lewcun, 'Bath Archaeological Trust News' from *The Survey of Bath & District No. 18*, November 2003. (BRO).
3. Translation from Charters of *Bath: Anglo-Saxon Charters 13* ed. S E Kelly, found on www.trin.cam.ac.uk/kemble/pelteret/Bath/Bath/%208.htm
4. See www.bathintime.co.uk photograph number 23271.
5. Mike Chapman, *The Lost Streams of Bath*. Survey of Old Bath, 2003. (BRO Acc. 0350/2/22/2).
6. Andrew Wright, *Court Hand Restored: A General Alphabet of Old Law Hands*. Plates 18 and 19. Published London, Reeves & Turner, 1879.
7. Bath City Waterworks File 152. (BRO).
8. Bath City Waterworks File 154. (BRO).
9. From the Bathampton Estate sale catalogue, 1921. Lot 2, [original] Bathampton House. (BRO).

From Rainfall to Reservoirs
Section II, Bathampton Waterworks and earlier sources

References:
10. *Somerset Record Society Proceedings* 'Mediaeval Deeds of Bath and District'. Vol. 73, part 2 – 300.3092/11&12. 1974. (BRO).
11. Bath Waterworks Act, 16 July 1846. (SA&LSS Ref. Q\RUP/182).
12. Seen in 2009 by members of the Bathampton Historic Buildings Survey.
13. *Bath Chronicle*, 17 April 1884. (BNA).
14. *Bath Chronicle*, 31 July 1943. (BNA).
15. From Records of the Oral History of Bathampton project. (BLHRG).
16. From Bathampton Historic Buildings Survey. (BLHRG).
17. Copy of Deeds held by BLHRG.
18. *Bath Chronicle*, 17 June 1886 – Letter from W J Wilcox. (BNA).
19. *Bristol Mercury*, 28 May 1886. (19th century Newspaper Archive).
20. *Bath Chronicle*, 3 June 1886 – Letter from Allen's agent Henry Spackman. (BNA).
21. Large Scale OS Maps – 1888, Sheet XIV6 and 1904, Sheet XIV6. (BRO).
22. Bathampton School Log Book 1863-1893. (SA&LSS).
23. Anna Grayson, *A Short History of Bathampton School, 1804-1990*. Pamphlet, nd. (BLHRG).
24. *Bath Chronicle*, 14 March 1914. (BNA).
25. Bath City Waterworks File Nos. 185 and 250. (BRO).
26. Sale Catalogue for the Bathampton Estate, 1921. (BRO).
27. *Bath Chronicle*, 5 June 1926. (BNA).
28. *Bath Chronicle,* 28 July 1934. (BNA).
29. *Bath Chronicle*, 2 December 1933. (BNA).
30. *Bath Chronicle*, 19 December 1936. (BNA).
31. Bath City Waterworks File 154. (BRO).
32. *Bath Chronicle*, 3 September 1938. (BNA).
33. Bath City Waterworks File 154. (BRO).
34. Bath City Waterworks File 258. (BRO).
35. *Bath Chronicle*, 3 June 1939. (BNA).
36. Bath City Waterworks File 258. (BRO).
37. Bath City Waterworks File 258. (BRO).

38. Bath City Waterworks File 258. (BRO).
39. Bath City Waterworks File 185. (BRO).
40. Bath City Waterworks File 185. (BRO).
41. Another source says only two garages were destroyed.
42. Bath City Waterworks File 258. (BRO).
43. Bath City Waterworks File Nos. 258 and 185. (BRO).
44. Bath City Waterworks File 243. (BRO).

From Rainfall to Reservoirs
Section III, Reservoirs on the Summit

References:

45. Bath City Waterworks File 15/8. (BRO).
46. John Rhodes, *Bath Golf Club – A History*. Publisher unknown, 2000.
47. Bath City Waterworks Files 15/8 and 15/8/i. (BRO).
48. *Bath Chronicle*, 3 June 1931 (cutting in Bath City Waterworks File No. 117/5ii). (BRO).
49. John Rhodes, *Bath Golf Club – A History*. Publisher unknown, 2000.
50. Bath City Waterworks File 117/8. (BRO).
51. *Bath and County Graphic,* June 1897. (BCL).
52. St Christopher's Close and Minster Way were built nearby in the late 1950s.
53. John Rhodes, *Bath Golf Club – A History*. Publisher unknown, 2000.
54. Brief outline of the History of the Waterworks Undertaking of Bath City Council 1900-31, 15 May 1931. Bath City Waterworks File 17/5ii. (BRO).
55. *Bath Chronicle*, 30 January 1932. (BNA).
56. *Water for a City*, by F G Warne, 1957. (BrRO Ref. BROFA/0144).
57. John Rhodes, *Bath Golf Club – A History*. Publisher unknown, 2000.

Sources:

Combe Down Waterworks Co. www.combedown.org and Combe Down Heritage Society.
Article in *Survey of Bath & District*, No 27, 2012. (BRO).
Bath City Waterworks Files Nos. 117/5i-iii; 117/7; 117/10; 117/13; 117/26/2-3; 193/1; 193/1i; 193/2i-ii; 193/9i-ii; 243; 243/2-3; 309. (BRO).

Postcript - The use of Bath Stone on the Down
Stone Gateposts, stiles and curios

References:

1. Article by A V Gandy in *Notes and Queries*, September 1938. (BCL).
2. See also Rod Thomas, *A Sacred Landscape, The Prehistory of Bathampton Down*. Millstream Books, 2008.

Illustrations

Front cover:

The photographer's twin sons looking across the old quarry workings from the north-east end of Bushy Norwood, c1920s. (© Bath in Time – G L Dafnis Collection, No. 338314. BCL).

Frontispiece: Bath, from Hampton Rocks (from a painting by A Heaton Cooper, c1927).

Back cover:

View over the old quarry workings with Batheaston and Bathford in the distance, c1920s. (© Bath in Time – G L Dafnis Collection, No. 336313. BCL).

Further Reading

Bathampton Footpaths Association –
   Walks around Bathampton, 2008

Boyce, Benjamin –
   The Benevolent Man. A Life of Ralph Allen of Bath.
   Harvard University Press, 1967.

Collinson, John –
   History and Antiquities of Somerset. 1791.

Egan, Pierce –
   Walks through Bath. Printed for Meyler and Son at the *Bath Herald* office, 1819

Oeynhausen, C Von, and, Dechen, H Von –
   Railways in England 1826 and 1827.
   Transcribed by E A Forward. Newcomen Society, 1971.

Rack, Edmund –
   Survey of Somerset, 1781-7.
   Republished by Somerset Archaeological Society, 2011.

Thomas, Rod –
   A Sacred Landscape. The Prehistory of Bathampton Down.
   Millstream Books, 2008.

Tunstall, James –
   Rambles Around Bath. 2nd Edition, 1848.

Index

Fig. numbers in bold